T0339108

Cambridge Elements ≡

Elements in Shakespeare Performance
edited by
W. B. Worthen
Barnard College

VIRAL SHAKESPEARE

Performance in the Time of Pandemic

Pascale Aebischer
University of Exeter

CAMBRIDGE
UNIVERSITY PRESS

CAMBRIDGE
UNIVERSITY PRESS

University Printing House, Cambridge CB2 8BS, United Kingdom

One Liberty Plaza, 20th Floor, New York, NY 10006, USA

477 Williamstown Road, Port Melbourne, VIC 3207, Australia

314–321, 3rd Floor, Plot 3, Splendor Forum, Jasola District Centre,
New Delhi – 110025, India

103 Penang Road, #05–06/07, Visioncrest Commercial, Singapore 238467

Cambridge University Press is part of the University of Cambridge.

It furthers the University's mission by disseminating knowledge in the pursuit of
education, learning, and research at the highest international levels of excellence.

www.cambridge.org
Information on this title: www.cambridge.org/9781108947961
DOI: 10.1017/9781108943482

First published 2021

A catalogue record for this publication is available from the British Library.

ISBN 978-1-108-94796-1 Paperback
ISSN 2516-0117 (online)
ISSN 2516-0109 (print)

Viral Shakespeare

Performance in the Time of Pandemic

Elements in Shakespeare Performance

DOI: 10.1017/9781108943482

First published online: December 2021

Pascale Aebischer

University of Exeter

Author for correspondence: Pascale Aebischer, p.v.aebischer@exeter.ac.uk

ABSTRACT: This Element offers a first-person phenomenological history of watching productions of Shakespeare during the pandemic year of 2020. The first section of the Element explores how Shakespeare 'went viral' during the first lockdown of 2020 and considers how the archival recordings of Shakespeare productions made freely available by theatres across Europe and North America impacted modes of spectatorship and viewing practices, with a particular focus on the effect of binge watching *Hamlet* in lockdown. The Element's second section documents two made-for-digital productions of Shakespeare by Oxford-based Creation Theatre and Northern Irish Big Telly, two companies that became leaders in digital theatre during the pandemic. It investigates how their productions of *The Tempest* and *Macbeth* modelled new platform-specific ways of engaging with audiences and creating communities of viewing at a time when, in the United Kingdom, government policies were excluding most non-building-based theatre companies and freelancers from pandemic relief packages.

This Element also has a video abstract: www.cambridge.org/aebischer

KEYWORDS: broadcast, digital, pandemic, performance, shakespeare

ISBNs: 9781108947961 (PB), 9781108943482 (OC)

ISSNs: 2516-0117 (online), 2516-0109 (print)

Contents

Introduction

Shakespeare Goes Viral

Imagine then that all this while, Death (like ... stalking *Tamberlaine*)
hath pitcht his tents ... in the sinfully-polluted Suburbes: the Plague is
Muster-maister and Marshall of the field: ... the maine Army consisting
(like *Dunkirke*) of a mingle-mangle.

(Thomas Dekker, 'The Wonderfull Yeare. 1603'. D1 r)

[T]he publick shew'd, that they would bear their Share in these Things;
the very Court, which was then Gay and Luxurious, put on a Face of just
Concern, for the publick Danger: All the Plays and Interludes ... were
forbid to Act ... for the Minds of the People, were agitated with other
Things; and a kind of Sadnes and Horror at these Things, sat upon the
Countenances, even of the common People.

(Daniel Defoe, *Journal of the Plague Year* [1722] 1992, pp. 28–9)[1]

In March 2020, theatres went dark and screens lit up across Western
Europe, Canada and the United States. In Exeter, United Kingdom, where
I live, people were hunkering down after a final week of frenzied attempts to
get supplies (of all things) of toilet roll, along with bulk purchases of hand
sanitiser, dried pasta and tinned tomatoes. Meanwhile in Staunton, Virginia,
the American Shakespeare Center's actors got together for one final performance of their touring production of *A Midsummer Night's Dream*.
Playing to an empty theatre and filmed by three camera operators who
were learning and visibly improving their craft skills in the course of the
performance, that production felt like a swansong: a last, desperately joyful,

---

[1] Defoe's *Journal*, written in 1722 about the plague year of 1665, when he was just
five years old, is not as much an eye-witness account as a fictional memoir, based
on extensive research, that offers a cautionary tale to contemporary readers at
a time when the next outbreak of the bubonic plague was thought to be imminent
(Backscheider, 1992).

cobbled-together tribute to an era of communal theatre making and theatre watching that had abruptly come to an end.[2]

As one country after another shut its entertainment industries, daily press conferences communicated infection and death rate statistics along with the latest sets of restrictions on everyday life, 'non-essential' workers were furloughed, left unemployed or made to convert their homes into workplaces. Care homes shut their doors and battled with outbreaks that killed many residents. Households went into isolation, parents struggled to combine work with homeschooling their children, and the silence outside our house deepened until birdsong could be heard again, punctured with alarming frequency by the howling of ambulances in the distance.

Locked out of their theatres, actors, managers, producers, backstage creatives and their legal teams leapt into action. Many big theatres that had, over the previous decade, started to extend their reach beyond their local communities by appealing to national and international audiences through digital theatre broadcasts, now rushed to adapt to the 'new normal' of isolation by hastily checking and renegotiating broadcast contracts so as to allow them to open up their archives. Audiences worldwide were given free access to past productions but were asked for donations to keep the institutions afloat. Other theatre companies, and freelance performers who rapidly organised into new configurations, retooled almost instantly to continue performing live via videoconferencing platforms, with the Zoom platform emerging as the most commonly used digital stage. Sir Patrick Stewart started to read one Shakespeare sonnet a day, and seasoned actors and novices alike performed monologues to their phone cameras.[3]

Audiences responded by binge watching Shakespeare productions brought into their homes from a range of theatrical cultures and to organise their diaries so as to accommodate the fortnightly *Globe on*

---

[2] Michelle Manning writes about this production in a draft chapter for *International Academic Arenas* (PhD thesis, Anglia Ruskin University).

[3] For fuller accounts of the range of Shakespeare productions around the world, see Allred and Broadribb (2022b); Kirwan and Sullivan (2020); Smith, Valls-Russell and Yabut (2020).

Screen streams from Shakespeare's Globe on Monday nights, the weekly live hybrid of Zoom-plus-YouTube performance from the *The Show Must Go Online* series on Wednesdays,[4] the Thursday double bill of streams by the Stratford Festival in Ontario and National Theatre At Home on YouTube, and the weekly *ALMOST live* Royal Shakespeare Company (RSC) show on Marquee T.V on Saturdays.[5] Companies with smaller archives, such as Cheek by Jowl or Lazarus Theatre, had to squeeze their own streams into this busy schedule. Those who, like me, have an interest in European theatre, additionally slotted in streams from many of the most prominent European houses. To help one another through the maze of available productions, bloggers began to create listings of English-language and European streams. Impromptu 'watch party' communities and Zoom discussion groups sprung up, while on Twitter, hashtags connected with specific streams pulled viewers together into audience groups on the hoof.

On social media, memes about how Shakespeare wrote *King Lear* and *Macbeth* while supposedly 'quarantined' during the plague began to spread and eventually got picked up by mainstream media. An allusive cartoon in *The New Yorker* magazine did not even need to mention Shakespeare to make its Shakespearean point (Figure 1). Instead, Maddie Dai made the link explicitly in the tweet with which she shared her cartoon on social media: 'devastated the pandemic has revealed yet another difference between shakespeare and i: he spends quarantine writing king lear, i spend quarantine writing panicked messages to my father, telling him to leave bunnings warehouse [sic]' (@maddiedai, 23 March 2020). Meanwhile, in a full-length article in *The Guardian*, Andrew Dickson trawled through *Romeo and Juliet, Timon of Athens* and *King Lear* to find the most repulsive plague metaphors that might have arisen from his direct experience of writing during outbreaks (2020).

In other words, Shakespeare, both as a cultural figure and in the shape of his plays, 'went viral'. Karine Nahon and Jeff Hemsley (2013, p. 16) define

---

[4] The series had started on Thursdays but moved to Wednesdays once the NT live shows began to screen on Thursdays.

[5] @TheRSC tweet, 10:20 a.m., 27 March 2020.

*"Day 6! Couldn't decide between starting to write my
novel or my screenplay, so instead I ate three boxes of mac
and cheese and then lay on the floor, panicking."*

Figure 1 'Day 6!' *New Yorker* cartoon, 23 March 2020. © Maddie Dai

such virality in media as 'a social information flow process where many
people simultaneously forward a specific information item, over a short
period of time, within their social networks, and where the message spreads
beyond their own [social] networks to different, often distant networks,
resulting in a sharp acceleration in the number of people who are exposed to
the message'. Shakespeare thus began to be associated with extraordinary
productivity and creative genius that was linked to the newly widespread
scenario of social isolation for fear of contagion. At the same time, he also
paradoxically became a figure for community at a time of isolation, and the
ability for art in general and theatre more specifically to reach beyond the
boundaries set up by lockdown conditions and connect artists with their
audiences and audiences with one another.

Celebrating Shakespeare in Lockdown

Just over a month into the United Kingdom's first Covid-19 lockdown, Shakespeare lovers across the world celebrated 'Shakespeare's birthday' on St George's Day, 23 April. This was a day spent entirely online as I launched *Shakespeare, Spectatorship and the Technologies of Performance*, a decidedly pre-pandemic book focused on the rapid expansion in the use of digital performance technologies between 2013 and 2016. Part III of the book, as it turned out, was suddenly highly topical in its concern with the question of how digital theatre broadcasting might create liveness effects for viewers distributed across the globe watching Shakespeare from their individual homes. I had vaguely planned a low-key local book launch sweetened with Devon scones, clotted cream and strawberry jam for my Exeter colleagues. Instead, I was now engaged in a social media campaign that involved a podcast alongside unreasonable amounts of tweeting in both the morning and the afternoon to catch the attention of potential European and North American audiences.

In between tweets to boost the Shakespeare birthday celebration posts of colleagues who were also launching books and giving lectures to mark the occasion, I rewatched parts of Toneelgroep Amsterdam's stream of its Dutch-language production of *Het Temmen van de Feeks/The Taming of the Shrew* (see pp. 43–52 of this Element) and dipped into the stream of *Hamlet* which had just come online the night before from the Maxim Gorki Theater in Berlin.

In the early afternoon, I participated in a crowdcast research seminar on early modern soundscapes. Then, in preparation for a group discussion on Zoom the next day of the National Theatre's YouTube broadcast of Simon Godwin's 2017 *Twelfth Night* starring Tamsin Greig as Malvolia, I rewatched parts of that *National Theatre At Home* broadcast. I took some time out at 8 p.m. to join the rest of the United Kingdom in the weekly ritual of the one-minute-long round of applause to show our appreciation of the tireless work and sacrifices made by the National Health Service and carers in dealing with the pandemic. I then returned to my screen.

As Europeans arrived towards the end of their Shakespeare celebrations and my family went to bed, more and more events were coming online from the United States.

First off the mark was the Folger Shakespeare Library, which had hosted a series of lecture and workshop streams during the afternoon and now 'premiered' a stream of its 2014 co-production of Teller and Aaron Posner's *Macbeth* as a 'watchalong' on its Facebook site. As a family of actors (Ian Merrill Peakes/Macbeth, Karen Peakes/Lady Macduff and their son) cheerily greeted their online audience and introduced the show, extreme fatigue kicked in at my end. Never having been able to see a Shakespeare production in the Folger theatre, I was thrilled to gain virtual access to this space. After a few minutes, however, my concentration began to falter and I got distracted by the little emojis bobbing up across the screen as the roughly 200 participants in the watchalong began to engage with the performance.

Even more distracting were the comments that started to appear on the side of the screen, which were largely phatic, communicating for the sake of communication. Many audience members were greeting one another and the performers, creating a lively dialogue and community of Folger Theatre fans from whom, in my tiredness, I felt increasingly detached and alienated. Having tuned in to connect and celebrate with North American audiences, I now found myself almost actively resisting connection because it was increasingly obvious that we were coming at supposedly the same thing – Shakespeare – from such different contexts and time zones. As they joyously discussed the kilts worn by the performers and admired the spookiness of Teller's magical artistry in creating the illusions that characterised the appearances of the production's witches and ghost, I felt ever more dissociated from their experience and communal appreciation.

It was a relief, at 11.30 p.m., to switch to the start of the Canadian watchalong party hosted by the Stratford Festival, Ontario. Here, I found Festival director Antoni Cimolino in a high-brow conversation with Colm Feore, the star of the *King Lear* stream that would start half an hour later. The change in atmosphere was disconcerting: the discussion now ranged from the challenges of playing a political leader to references to current US politics in what turned out to be the final months of the Trump presidency. In stark contrast with the chummy gregariousness of the Folger watchalong, no attempt was made to interact directly with the *King Lear* audience: this was a carefully curated conversation between elite creatives that viewers were privileged to observe rather than invited to participate in.

When the stream of *King Lear* began, the time had finally come for my final anniversary engagement: the 'viewing party' of the National Theatre's *Twelfth Night* for North American audiences, hosted by the Shakespeare Theatre Company at the Harman Center for the Arts on its brand-new streaming platform, 'Shakespeare Everywhere', and featuring Simon Godwin, the production's director. I was curious about how Godwin would frame his very British production for his American audience. I was also keen to find out whether the kind of veneration of Shakespeare and authenticity that had marked the Folger's watchalong party would also be evident at this other anniversary event hosted by a venue in Washington, DC. Having equipped myself with a fresh pot of tea and some snacks, I switched to the site – and found the event had been cancelled due to unforeseen technical problems.

'And so to bed', as Pepys might say.

Viral Shakespeare: A Journal of the Pandemic Year

> I have set this particular down so fully, because I know not but it may be of Moment to those who come after me, if they come to be brought to the same Distress, and to the same manner of making their Choice.
>
> (Daniel Defoe, *Journal of the Plague Year* [1722] 1992, p. 11)

My personal experience of Shakespeare's birthday, at the peak of the first wave of the Covid-19 pandemic, explains some of the features of this Element, researched and written distractedly and under uniquely pressured conditions during two periods of lockdown, in April to May and November to December 2020. A final retrospective phase of writing and editing was squeezed into May and June 2021, when I was in quarantine for seventeen days. From this vantage point, it is striking just how quickly people are adapting to ever-new situations and are eager to move on from the shock of the first lockdown and leave those memories behind: all the talk is of a roadmap to lifting all restrictions and starting a 'new normal'. This, in turn, provides an urgent incentive for finishing this Element while I am still capable of remembering what lockdown *felt* like. Rather than a piece of formal scholarship, therefore, this Element is conceived as a phenomenological history of sorts of watching Shakespeare in this first pandemic year in which I share my responses to some of the unique spectatorial configurations, novel experiences and creative innovations that emerged in the time of pandemic.

In the first lockdown (25 March to July 2020), I binge watched Shakespeare whenever I was not teaching and looking after a cohort of desperately needy and disoriented students who had been sent home mid-term, or doing my bit to clean, wash, cook and care for my family, while also planting potatoes and vegetables in case of food shortages (yes, life really felt that precarious – a year down the line, it seems absurd). Work bled into family life and leisure became work. As restrictions were eased, I spent five months investigating how two British companies, Creation Theatre (Oxford) and Big Telly (Northern Ireland) had managed to pivot from analogue to digital modes of theatre production in record time. The *Digital Toolkit* I produced with Rachael Nicholas was designed to throw a lifeline to other creatives in the theatre industry by helping them with their own digital transformations.[6] As winter approached again and we entered a second lockdown on 31 October, my teenagers were back at school and my students were back at university. Writing time was snatched between asynchronous online teaching and hybrid face-to-face-plus-Zoom classroom sessions.

Accordingly, this Element is written from within the conditions of lockdown, with all that this implies in terms of limited access to all non-digital sources of information, human contact, haircuts, physical exercise and uninterrupted time. It is also written, at breakneck speed in intermittent bursts, from a retrospective viewpoint that is informed by my early modernist's immersion in the past and my current work with researchers

---

[6] *Digital Theatre Transformation: A Case Study and Digital Toolkit for Small to Mid-scale Theatres in England* was a 'rapid-response' Covid-19 research project I undertook with Rachael Nicholas that was funded by the Arts and Humanities Research Council in the United Kingdom between May and October 2020.

committed to analysing and mitigating the effects of the pandemic.[7] Its main focus is the two months following the British prime minister's announcement of the closure of the theatres on 23 March 2020. This first lockdown saw the most viral outbreak of Shakespeare-inspired activity that peaked, almost to absurdity, on that memorable birthday celebration on 23 April, and which began to subside at the end of May, with the arrival of summer. It is, in many ways, a personal memoir of that period, which just a few months later seems already a world away.

In the first part of this Element dedicated to theatre broadcasts of Shakespeare during the first lockdown, therefore, my purpose is twofold. On the one hand, it is to document the extraordinary shift, within the shortest time frame, of Shakespeare performance from a predominantly analogue, communal experience in a single space and time to the almost exclusively digital production, dissemination and consumption of Shakespeare performance as the new norm. That documentation cannot be exhaustive and is of necessity limited to the handful of productions that stood out for me, nor can it be anything but subjective and limited by the languages that I speak or have any hope of understanding, the time zone I inhabit and the professional and social networks to which I have access.

On the other hand, my purpose is to examine the impact this shift has had on the experience of Shakespeare performance. The question of why Shakespeare became such a particularly striking focal point for cultural activity can probably be answered with reference to the need to group around something familiar that carries cultural capital at moments of crisis. A more sophisticated answer might involve pointing out how Shakespeare's plays themselves 'insistently draw on the metaphorics of communicable disease, or make direct allusions to the plague itself and its concomitant quarantine and self-isolation restrictions' (Ristani 2020). More prosaically and realistically, the playwright's convenient copyright status, his inclusion as a compulsory element of secondary education in the United Kingdom

---

[7] *The Pandemic and Beyond: The Arts and Humanities Contribution to Covid-19 Research and Recovery* is a research coordination project funded by the Arts and Humanities Research Council; it is running between March 2021 and February 2023.

and the ready availability of Shakespeare in the archives of companies certainly had a role to play in his prominence at this time. What interests me more is the question of how the change in the viewing context and the sheer concentration of broadcast Shakespeares altered both the experience of viewing and the productions themselves.

What happened when different performance cultures were brought into abrupt collision? To what extent and how did viewing communities bond through their common love of Shakespeare within and across time zones? How did the pressure of viewing schedules lend a structure to life in the groundhog-day experience of lockdown? What happened when so many broadcasts of a single play coincided that they began to lose their distinctiveness? Could a live stream from an empty theatre conjure up the ghosts of the past and bridge the gap between the living and the dead? If Shakespeare was the food of love, was there excess of it?

From the vantage point of the second lockdown, in which watch parties had largely disappeared and no more streams were made available by the main broadcast companies, the second part of this Element explores the emergence of the commercial Zoom videoconferencing platform as a new live performance stage. At the heart of this section is the work of Creation Theatre and Big Telly, the two companies that have worked together to co-produce some of the most innovative professional Zoom performances of that period. I consider their *Tempest* – possibly the very first professional Shakespeare production to be reshaped for Zoom performance in April 2020 – and Big Telly's Halloween show of *Macbeth* (October 2020), which virtually 'toured' from Belfast to Oxford, where it had a 'residency' with Creation Theatre.

Here, my purpose is to share some of the insights gained from working with Creation Theatre and with Zoë Seaton, the Director of Big Telly, in the summer of 2020 and to map out some of the challenges faced by freelancers in the theatre industry as they confronted an industrial and cultural landscape in which Shakespeare was understood as a common good who should be freely accessible for all, even as creatives were not being paid for their labour. Additionally, I reflect on the affordances of the Zoom platform as a digital stage. How do the platform and its audiences remediate and 'archive' the experience of live theatre? How do Zoom's affordances and the hybrid of theatre, television and videoconferencing open up new ways of exploring Shakespeare's spatial dramaturgy and the spectator-performer relationships of the early modern stage? To what extent did these productions facilitate an experience of community and virtual co-presence? What remnants of theatricality survive within this medium?

Together, the two sections of the Element document the form and pressure of a time in which Shakespeare became the mirror image and cultural antidote to the virus that attacked us. The fleeting insights and experiences garnered from watching Shakespeare in lockdown are worth preserving because they speak to a moment of unprecedented intensity and emotional rawness that is profoundly marked by Shakespeare. Shakespeare emerges from this period as a common reference point and source of comfort, as well as a focal point for community building and manic cultural activity even as the economy went into hibernation. His currency swelled as the contagion took root; it ebbed off as we got used to living with the threat and news of a vaccine brought hope of physical, cultural and economic recovery. Whether as a means to channel grief and anxiety or share laughter and a dogged insistence on shared experiences, culture, creativity and survival, the viral Shakespeare of 2020 constitutes a profound incision in our performance culture that will forever divide pre- from post-pandemic performance, even as it already risks receding into the indistinct past.

Remember thee?
Ay, thou poor ghost, whiles memory holds a seat
In this distracted globe. (*Hamlet* 1.5.95–97).

1 Archival Obsessions

But I must go back again to the Beginning of this Surprizing Time, while the Fears of the People were young.

(Daniel Defoe, *Journal of the Plague Year* [1722] (1992), p. 20)

At the end of March 2020, just days after the theatres were forced to close, the Schaubühne in Berlin set up a digital theatre programme under the title 'coercive measures', which implied a strong-arming of the audience into submitting itself to a regime that promised to combat the virus not through restrictions on movement and the gathering of people but through the forcefully imposed consumption of theatre. As so often, the German version of the title managed to convey an even more complex set of concepts: *Zwangsvorstellungen* is a pun which can mean 'obsession' or 'delusion' on the one hand and 'performances under duress' or 'forced entertainment' on the other. The title of the programme was thus uncannily prescient of some of the psychological effects of compulsion, obsession and delusion that would be provoked by the deluge of live streams that audiences submitted themselves to, captive in their own homes.

The Shakespeare play which archival streams most readily used as a means of speaking to the present moment was *Hamlet*, the only one of Shakespeare's tragedies to take place in a sort of lockdown, as Hamlet is trapped in Elsinore, unable to return to the freedom of his student life in Wittenberg. Hamlet emerges as the archetypal hero whose desire for action and resistance is frustrated by the fundamental rot that has taken hold of his environment. Hamlet himself is the victim of what, anachronistically, we might recognise as a viral contagion of his memory bank when he promises to 'wipe away all trivial fond records' 'from the table of [his] memory' to store in it only the (potentially destructive) information transmitted to him by the Ghost (1.5.98–99).

As J. F. Bernard recognises, furthermore, *Hamlet* as a play itself has the potential to be contagious and 'viral' in its dissemination. In the same manner in which anti-theatrical writers thought of theatres as places of accelerated plague contagion, Bernard suggests, the play of *Hamlet*, by virtue of its hero's final injunction that his story be told, initiated a chain of transmission involving theatregoers

> carrying Hamlet's story with them and introducing it to different spheres. The play closes with the hope that specta-tors will uphold this bond and tell his story. . . . The cycle is indeed, plague-like: the story of Hamlet leaps off the stage, spreads through the bawdy playhouse, and escapes the sinful suburbs to finally reach the homes of unsuspecting relatives

who fall victim to the invisible narratives that theatregoers
carried home with them. (2019, p. 225)

Hamlet, in other words, is a play that was written to 'go viral' long before
a viral pandemic accelerated its digital dissemination yet further.

The blurb for the stream of Kay Voges' 2014 production at the
Schauspielhaus Dortmund explained the suitability of this particular play
for the contexts of 2014 and 2020 as follows:

> 'The time is out of joint': ... William Shakespeare paints
> a world on the brink in which paranoia, doubt and loneliness
> lurk. His tragedy, like a seismograph, listens to the tremors
> of the present (in any place, at any time) – and asks the
> question how one should continue to live in a world that has
> been shaken in its foundations ... this Dortmund *Hamlet* of
> 2014 asks the question about being and not being in the
> global digital age. What exactly is it that threatens to con-
> sume everyone and everything? What are the diseases of the
> present? How can we fight them? And: what would
> a production of *Hamlet* look like in the spring of 2020?

It is some of these topics – the sense of out-of-jointness, despair,
isolation, disease and mourning, and the question of how archived productions looked when they were redeployed in the spring of 2020 – that I want
to think about in relation to some of the *Hamlet*-related broadcasts that
I exposed myself to under ever greater pressure. Between 1 April and 5 May,
I watched ten broadcasts of Shakespeare's *Hamlet* (including *Fratricide
Punished*) and Heiner Müller's *Hamletmaschine* while also absorbing
streams of a range of other productions of texts by Shakespeare (*Richard
III*, *Shrew*, *Coriolanus*, *Macbeth*, *Much Ado*, *Merchant*, *Dream*, *Tempest*),
Schiller, Brecht, Zweig, Birch and Ibsen. In the final part of this section,
I move away from considering the effects of binge watching *Hamlet* to the
opposite type of engagement with a lockdown Shakespeare stream: the
obstinate effort to watch and rewatch an initially incomprehensible Dutch
production over a three-month period.

1.1 Binge Watching Hamlet *in Lockdown*

Bad Dreams: Watching Thomas Ostermeier's *Hamlet* Jangled Out of Tune, and Harsh (1 April 2020)

[M]any … lock'd themelves up, and kept hid till the Plague was over; and many Families foreseeing the Approach of the Distemper, laid up Stores of Provisions, sufficient for their whole Families, and shut themselves up, and that so entirely, that they were neither seen or heard of, till the Infection was quite ceased.

(Daniel Defoe, *Journal of the Plague Year* [1722] 1992, p. 49)

My *Hamlet* binge began with Thomas Ostermeier's *Hamlet*, streamed online on 1 April 2020 between 6.30 p.m. and midnight (GMT+2) as one of the first of the Schaubühne's programme of *Zwangsvorstellungen*. I asked to be excused from the dinner table and from bedtime routines, retreated to the spare room that was now my 'office' and settled down for the first of a series of evenings of both being and not being at home, being and not being at work. Ignoring the sounds of family life in the background, I watched the stream one and a half times during the tight streaming window. As I did so, I furiously took notes, while also keeping an eye on the live tweets of colleagues, friends and strangers whom I had joined for what turned out to be the first of many Shakespeare watch parties in lockdown.

Having got to the end of my first viewing, I quickly wrote a short Twitter thread to share some of the observations I had made, in the hope of some feedback from watch party members (see Figure 2). Tellingly, that thread was largely invisible to the other people in the watch party because, having been schooled in German, I put an *Umlaut* ('ue' for 'ü') into #SchaubuehneHamlet. Meanwhile, all the other watch party members used the anglicised hashtag #SchaubuhneHamlet. With the hashtags out of joint, my experience of the watch party was one in which I was writing into the void and disconnected from the group whose chatter I was avidly reading – divergence, not convergence; isolation, not community.

Just finished watching #SchaubuehneHamlet. Hugely thought-provoking as a production, and also interesting from a broadcasting point of view. Did anyone else spot the rapid reverse zoom on Claudius' prayer, pushing him away from the viewer? Same as in Robin Lough's Hamlet for RSC.

9:19 PM · Apr 1, 2020 · Twitter Web App

ılı View Tweet activity

1 Retweet   5 Likes

♡   ↻   ♡   ⬆

Pascale Aebischer @PascaleExeter · Apr 1   •••
Replying to @PascaleExeter
Also some interesting effects breaking through the fourth wall as suddenly Hamlet steps out of the illusion in direct address to the audience/the sound technicians to ask for the music to be stopped and the camera shows him from the point of view of someone on the stage behind.

♡ 1   ↻   ♡   ⬆   ılı

Pascale Aebischer @PascaleExeter · Apr 1   •••
So there's an effort, in the camerawork, to reinforce some of the production choices. I need to do a lot more thinking and a bit of re-viewing before I can settle on what I make of it all. Certainly an extraordinary amount of dirt-eating!

♡ 1   ↻   ♡ 1   ⬆   ılı

Pascale Aebischer @PascaleExeter · Apr 1   •••
Just a final note: I watched this in German, no English subtitles. And, as with watching @CbyJ Revenger's in Italian a few weeks ago, I was struck by the immediacy and colloquialism/crudeness (in a good way) of the translation, which made me pay attention as if this were all new.

♡ 1   ↻   ♡   ⬆   ılı

Pascale Aebischer @PascaleExeter · Apr 1   •••
(I do wonder what the experience was like for Anglophones who were relying on the subtitles - @Profrob83, here's thinking of your work on this!). How modern did the subtitles feel?

♡ 3   ↻   ♡   ⬆   ılı

Pascale Aebischer @PascaleExeter · Apr 1   •••
Afterthought: so the language was as dirty as Hamlet himself.

♡   ↻   ♡ 1   ⬆   ılı

Figure 2 Twitter thread, 1 April 2020

From the very start, the broadcast intensified the disjunctions that characterise both the world of the play and the situation of lockdown viewing. No effort was made to recontextualise the stream for a 2020 audience; instead the stream was transparently a rebroadcast of the live broadcast from the Festival of Avignon on 18 July 2008 on ARTE, the European culture TV channel. That original context was emphasised through the inclusion of a pre-performance interview with Ostermeier, who was visibly younger and more awkwardly sheepish than the imposing figure I had met at a conference in 2014. The pre-show chat firmly located the stream in the 'here-and-now' of Avignon in the summer of 2008 and the excitement of the two thousand viewers in the Court of Honour of the Popes' Palace.

Yet it also spoke, with an exciting sense of anachronistic friction, to the experience of watching the stream on my home office computer. As Ostermeier pointed out that the setting of the play in a fortress resonated with the high walls surrounding Popes' Palace, the site sensitivity of the production in the Avignon setting easily translated into a sensitivity to the lockdown situation from which I was watching. When Ostermeier then went on to point to the sky over the open-air venue to explain how the firmament above allows performers to know what they are talking about when they mention the heavens, that in turn made me yet more conscious of being locked into a room inside my house, unable to be part of the tiered wall of spectators waiting for the performance to start on a warm summer evening.

Similarly, the director's pointed remarks about the geographical and cultural dislocations that saw a play set in a Danish fortress performed in the South of France for a Francophone audience in German only worked to highlight the ways in which the lockdown had brought communities from across Europe together to watch this broadcast, with audiences able to choose subtitling in either French or English. Awareness of the privilege of international access to a broadcast that had previously only ever been shown on German and French television was part of the excitement of this event for those of us who had previously only been able to read about, but not see, this landmark production.

In normal circumstances, Margaret Jane Kidnie (2018, p. 134) explains, theatre broadcasts involve a mutual reaching out: the 'spectator's technology-enabled body reaches out to engage in the moment with the actors' reciprocally-enabled bodies, troubling a seemingly self-evident boundary between presence and absence premised on the conjunction of body, place, and time' (2018, p. 134). Such a virtual meeting in the middle was both encouraged and ultimately frustrated by the situation of lock-down. Encouraged because of the ways in which the Schaubühne opened up the access to its stream across different European languages and the speed at which we assembled into a watch party. But frustrated, too, by the disjunc-tion between the frame of the *Zwangsvorstellungen* in lockdown and the clearly pre-Covid circumstances of the Avignon Festival, with its two thousand spectators rubbing shoulders and also between myself, with my out-of-synch hashtag, and the rest of the watch party. If we were reaching out, we were doing so in different directions, reaching into the void for much of the time.

'*Sein oder Nichtsein, das ist die Frage.*' Having chosen to forgo the mediation of subtitles, the opening of the performance with these iconic words – the first of three iterations of Hamlet's soliloquy – jolted me. Not only were they 'in the wrong place' within the play, but these were 'the wrong words': German, not English, and missing the '*hier*' that is iconic in German thanks to the currency of August Wilhelm von Schlegel's rendering as '*Sein oder Nichtsein; das ist hier die Frage*' (3.1.59). Instead of the canonical feminine line ending, with its qualifica-tion of *hier*/here that restricts Hamlet's dilemma to his specific situation at that moment, this was a regular, more forceful pentameter line. The question was universal and urgent – rather like the First Quarto's startling 'To be, or not to be, I there's the point' that, in its purposeful regularity, has a similar capacity to make us hear the question with fresh ears and urgency.

As the performance wore on, I repeatedly found myself mentally translating the text of the fast-paced German dialogue in Marius von Mayenburg's electrifyingly contemporary translation of Shakespeare's play back into English. Doing so brought home, for the first time, how remarkably crude Shakespeare's play is in its register, but in a way that has been mellowed by the patina of age that encases a text that is too, too familiar to shock. In von Mayenburg's translation, mad Ophelia's references to being 'tumbled' and having 'come to my bed' are like bells jangled, out of tune and harsh, as she complains of having been 'screwed' (*'gevögelt'*) and 'fucked' (*'gefickt'*).

The brutal immediacy of the linguistic register that pulled me into the *now* of the production was, paradoxically, also what made the viewing experience one of intense linguistic hypermediacy, which incorporated a heterogeneity of languages, creating a rich linguistic sensorium in my head. I found myself performing multiple acts of linguistic mediation: imagining what it must have been like for the Francophone Avignon audience to read the French surtitles which were not visible in the broadcast, barely consciously running the English text in my head, while intently listening to the German.

All the while, I was also remembering Robert Shaughnessy's analysis of the English surtitles of Marius von Mayenburg's 'punchy, vernacular prose' translation of Shakespeare for Ostermeier's production of *Richard III* (Shaughnessy 2020, p. 48), which I had recently read in draft form to help with some of the translations. Shaughnessy's research explores the process through which the German text of that production was rendered into English in a way that made an effort to close the gap to Shakespeare's text while also adapting the length of the lines to make them suitable as surtitles.

Thus, in one example Shaughnessy cites from *Richard III*, von Mayenburg's

> *'Jetzt wurde der Winter unsrer Erniedrigung zu strahlendem Sommer durch diesen Sohn der Yorks, und all die Wolken, die sich türmten gegen unser Haus, sind tief im Meeresgrund versenkt'*

would, in a literal retranslation into English, be

> 'The winter of our humiliation has now become a radiant summer through this son of [the] York[s], and all the clouds that have piled up against our house are sunk deep in the seabed.' (Shaughnessy, 2020, p. 49)

The German text combines a certain formality that preserves the 'feel' of watching classical drama with a modern diction and word choices that make it easier for a present-day performer and audience to relate to the emotion. As Shaughnessy points out, substituting '*Erniedrigung*' – so, 'humiliation' or 'degradation' – for 'discontent' is what gives von Mayenburg's text a 'contemporary flavour' (Shaughnessy, 2020, p. 50).

However, instead of preserving that flavour of emotional rawness and directness of register for an Anglophone audience, the English surtitles for *Richard III* opted not so much for a retranslation of the German into English than for a barely perceptible compression of Shakespeare's famous opening lines into

> 'Now is the winter of our discontent
> made glorious summer
> by this sun of York.
>
> The clouds
> that lour'd upon our house
>
> In the deep bosom
> of the ocean buried.' (Shaughnessy, 2020, p. 51)

Similarly, for in the broadcast of *Hamlet*, a watch party participant confirmed, in answer to my question about how modern the translation felt, that 'about 95% of [the subtitle text] was just pulling straight from Shakespeare . . . and then 5% is Hamlet calling his mom a hot slut and other added colloquialisms' (Alex Heeney/@bwestcineaste, 2 April 2020). By the sound of it, that translation, too, compressed Shakespeare's text, with minor concessions to the 'feel' of the production's script, rather than offering a comprehensive retranslation of von Mayenburg's modern German text.[8]

---

[8] Rewatching a rented version of the performance with subtitles confirms that the English translation was predominantly based on Shakespeare's text, with occasional departures that introduced obscenities and colloquialisms, and occasional gaps that left out chunks of the German text.

Awareness of Shaughnessy's analysis of Ostermeier's *Richard III* surtitles increased my sense of disconnection and isolation but also my excitement at hearing Shakespeare out of tune and harsh, perhaps, but also *really hearing* the words in a way that wrenched me out of the torpor of overfamiliarity and into renewed, exciting openness to the play *as new writing*. This was my first German *Hamlet*, I was for the very first time hearing Shakespeare's lines in a language I had left behind more than twenty years before, and the freshness of it, the rawness and urgency was close to overwhelming. I knew that the people with whom I was virtually watching the performance were reading a somewhat different, more conservative and lulling version of the text from the one that I was hearing. German, which jumped at me with such vivid clarity and novelty, was likely to be little more than harsh background noise to many of them, a soundtrack of emotion rather than meaning. I also knew that with my rusty German, I was hearing the play in a way that was also different from how audiences in Germanophone Europe were hearing it.

The combination of isolation and awareness of the uniqueness of my circumstances produced a viewing experience that was of unprecedented intensity. I felt profoundly alive and present in that moment, and profoundly alone, dislodged from my home, my viewing companions, the audience in Avignon, and the production itself. Instead, I inhabited a utopian space of intensive presence: a hypermedial intercultural virtual environment shaped by the singular confluence of circumstances, preparation, linguistic skill sets and cultural competencies that I was uniquely placed to draw on in that particular way.

Rather than replicating, for the lockdown situation, an experience of connectedness and viewing community akin to that experienced as a physical theatre audience, therefore, my first watch party in lockdown, because of the disparity of our linguistic access to the production, resulted in an intercultural experience in which I floated alone, overstimulated and with a heady sense of disconnection from my environment that was matched by the glory of the intense connection to *this* Hamlet, in *this* language, at *this* time. I may have been watching synchronously with others, but despite my attempts to communicate with them and feel part of a community of viewers, the experience was one of having a parallel experience that could never quite connect with that of my watch party friends with whom I was in a constant state of dissonance rather than harmony.

In the middle of the broadcast, the production's obsession with the dirt on the floor of the stage which Hamlet rolled around in, ate, and into which he flung his interlocutors, briefly yielded to a sense of release from such bodily contagion when Hamlet reflected on how he might count himself a 'king of infinite space' even if 'bounded in a nutshell'. As Eidinger threw out his arms and the camera switched from a close-up to the most distant wide-angle shot that reduced the bright rectangle of the stage to a diminutive shape under the night sky, his voice reverberated over two thousand hushed spectators. Soaring high above the production, my own form of disembodied eagle-eyed viewpoint, I was exhilarated by my ability to bridge different cultures and languages, giddily dislocated in the contemporary nowhere/everywhere of that moment.

When Eidinger's Hamlet added the afterthought 'were it not that I have bad dreams' and the shot reverted to a close-up, the claustrophobia of lockdown and feeling of compression returned with renewed intensity. Now I was alone.

Arriving at the end, I wrote my thread of tweets and started watching the production over again. '*Sein oder Nichtsein, das ist die Frage . . .* '

Zwangsvorstellung: delusion, obsession, forced entertainment.

1.1.1 A 'Mingle-Mangle' Meshwork of *Hamlet*s (or: Screaming in the Void)

The bilingualism of the Schaubühne's programme and the fact that many of the streams included the options of English and French subtitles signals one of the most striking features of the opening up of the archives throughout German-speaking Europe: its appeal to an audience beyond its language community. The Schaubühne's subtitles were like a hand reaching across a cultural and political divide, offering a connection at a time when many Germans and UK nationals were intensely smarting from the legal separation between Britain and the EU that had just occurred in January 2020. They functioned like a virtual bridge in time and space that enabled retrospective cultural access to mainland Europe at a time when travel restrictions made physical access impossible.

Along with many other theatre audiences in the United Kingdom who had only been able to access the work of German directors and dramaturgs through touring productions that never seemed to travel any closer than distant London, I avidly seized on the opportunity to immerse myself in German-language theatre. With the time profoundly out of joint, I sat at my screen in Exeter and spent my days in Berlin, Bochum, Hamburg and Vienna. For the first time in decades, I sometimes dreamed in German.

The sense of intense out of jointness I experienced when watching these broadcasts came not only from my sense of mental dislocation from my physical location as my mind travelled to and settled in Germany and Austria but also from the disjointed way in which, as more productions became available for a limited duration within a short time frame, I increasingly found myself watching segments of different productions out of sequence. Rather like the indiscriminate 'mingle-mangle' of Death's army in Dekker's description of the plague of 1603 (D1 r), or his title page's promise of 'certaine Tales . . . cut out in sundry fashions, of purpose to shorten the liues of long winters nights, that lye watching in the darke for vs', the endless days of lockdown were shortened by a confluence of *Hamlet* streams that converged into an indiscriminate torrent. I stopped taking notes and just watched what I could while cooking; working out; at my desk; on my phone; interrupted by children, emails, or the latest statistics of contaminations and deaths on the news. Following that first stream of Ostermeier's *Hamlet*, my mode of viewing became ever more incoherent, distracted, pressurised, taking me beyond what I had the capacity to absorb, let alone digest.

Viewing in this way also involved the time being out of joint in another sense, as Peter Kirwan and Erin Sullivan (2020, p. 3) point out:

> [T]he temporal dislocations of a lockdown have complicated . . . the normal passage of time. Past productions are present; present productions disappear after limited periods; a production remains available while the experience of watching it at a moment of crisis passes; memories of earlier viewings blur with a fresh visit.

In other words, while binge watching is certainly something that has always been possible and has often been the experience of researchers and fans watching as many productions of a single play as possible in a short time span, three factors made the experience of binge watching in lockdown unique. The first is the time-limited availability of many streams that forced viewers into watching under pressure. The second is the fact that unlike the binge watching of DVDs and archival recordings that is normally a private, 'lone ranger' activity, much of the watching during lockdown was a communal activity, with groups virtually gathering to watch and discuss performances together, thus increasing the psychological pressure to keep up with other Shakespeare fans, friends and colleagues (what my teenagers might call #FOMO – fear of missing out). The third is the lockdown context itself, which made temporal and work-life boundaries disappear and made one day melt into the next. Together, the limited availability, peer pressure and dissolution of boundaries contributed to a mode of viewing that was quite unlike any other I'd previously experienced, even as a professional Shakespeare-watcher.

My increasingly chaotic viewing habits involved jumping back and forth between time periods and locations or, rather, folding productions originating from different time periods onto and into one another. I watched Robert Wilson's seminal production of Heiner Müller's *Hamletmaschine* of 1986 (a Thalia Theater Hamburg stream) on 1 May while I was still coming to terms with the stream of the made-for-lockdown restaging of Dimiter Gotscheff's production of *Hamletmaschine* that had been made available the week before (by the Deutsches Theater Berlin). As I was still taking in Wilson's extraordinarily stylised choreography in segments – I never had the concentration or time it would have taken to watch this demanding, loopingly repetitive, stream in one go – I was already moving on to the 2020 performance of Shakespeare's *Hamlet* directed by Johan Simons for the Schauspielhaus Bochum in 2019. Watching that broadcast, which was filmed at the start of lockdown without an audience, I was drawn back into the soundscape of the two *Hamletmaschine* streams I was still digesting, as Shakespeare's *Hamlet* was interrupted, at several points in the production, by passages inserted from Müller's adaptation.

Rather than experience these three iterations of *Hamletmaschine* as separate productions, therefore, they were like threads that folded into one another to become a dense, tangled, meshwork of German engagements with Shakespeare's and Müller's plays. The fabric of that meshwork was uneven: in some areas, the threads were tightly tangled together, whereas other parts of it spread out thinly in disparate directions, with no connection and offering no hold. The fabric made sensible, in a heightened way, the 'thick' areas onto which the streams converged and which themselves became tangled up by other broadcasts which I was also watching during that period, regardless of their thematic connection.

My point is this: as anthropologist Tim Ingold observes of the 'lines' traced by the movement of people through space, there is a distinction between a 'network', which consists of interconnected dots in space that allow a traveller to go from one place to the next, with each place important in itself (the destination is the focus, not the journey to it) and a 'meshwork'. Ingold describes how '[t]he lines of the meshwork' created by people as they move through space 'are the trails *along* which life is lived. And . . . it is in the entanglement of lines, not in the connecting of points, that the mesh is constituted' (Ingold 2007, p. 91, emphasis in original). Meshwork, in other words, is not static but processual, not organised but as haphazard as Dekker's 'mingle-mangle'. It is created by people as they move through space (whether physical or virtual, as in my movement through the *Hamlet* streams). It is constituted not of joints or knots, but of tangles; there are no dots, but convergences. And to experience the meshwork, you have to inhabit it in the manner of Ingold's wayfarer: his inhabitant 'participates from within in the very process of the world's continual coming into being'; 'in laying a trail of life, [the wayfarer] contributes to its weave and texture. These lines are typically winding and irregular, yet comprehensively entangled into a close-knit tissue' (Ingold 2007, pp. 91–2).

The out-of-jointness of this kind of meshwork frustrates any attempt to order the streams chronologically in one's mind, and to attempt the kind of diachronic mode of understanding the performance history of a play as a thread connecting with other threads in tidy knots of progressive inter-theatrical allusion. Instead, disjointed viewing smudges the clarity of chronological order and creates an anachronic meshwork that tangles the linear thread of time so as to bring different points in it together. Time periods and vectors of influence are rearranged in a manner defined by the serendipity of the viewer's trajectory through the material rather than by features intrinsic to the material: the viewer inhabits the material and, by virtue of their movement through it, creates the tangles of the meshwork. The meshwork exists because of this movement; it shifts and evolves. The perspective is one in which intertheatrical borrowings and allusions are not the effect of a pre-existing connection between productions, but of the viewer's travels through them. This brings with it the possibility of time-lines being reversed, so that a later production is perceived to be influencing an earlier staging.

Along with the transformation of linear timelines into meshworks, productions from different cultures and time periods are unexpectedly brought into dialogue. In the distracted globe of lockdown viewing, an extraordinary concentration of versions of the same thing from different parts of the globe converge in a single consciousness. Because there are too many *Hamlet*s in too few days, always on the same screen in the endless 'nowness' of the Internet's information streams turned deluge (what Ian Bogost terms the '*feed* of now, now, now' (Bogost 2010, p. 28)), the concentration of versions distracts the viewer from the thing they are watching at that moment as their mind wanders through the various versions, seeing new connections as the versions bleed into and contaminate one another. In the synchronicity that is a feature of the viral environment, the rules of diachronic influence make way for anachronicity. The broad-casts intersect and impact one another so that precursors turn into succes-sors, what follows after can change the meaning of what comes before, and dialogues between productions defy the laws of chronology. The linearity of succession makes way for viral interpenetration, as contagion travels freely between any broadcasts that come into contact.

Writing about the intertheatrical exchanges that allowed motifs from Renaissance Italian theatre to travel to England and become an integral part of Shakespearean dramaturgy, Louise George Clubb explains how 'the interchange and transformation of units, figures, relationships, actions, topoi, and framing patterns, gradually buil[t] a combinatory of theatergrams that were at once streamlined structures for svelte play making and elements of high specific density, weighty with significance from previous incarna-tions' (Clubb, 1989, p. 6). What lockdown facilitates is not so much the travel of such theatregrams as the co-opting of existing motifs which are pulled from across historically, geographically, textually separate sources into an enmeshment that gives them the theatregram's 'high specific density, weighty with significance'.

It is because of this that Heiner Müller's *Hamletmaschine* became ever more enmeshed with Shakespeare's *Hamlet*. Listening to Valery Tscheplanowa, in Dimiter Gotscheff's *Hamletmaschine*, talk about how '[t]he dance becomes wilder and wilder. Laughter from the coffin. On a swing a Madonna with breast-cancer. Horatio opens an umbrella, embraces Hamlet. Freeze in the embrace under the umbrella', the image of Tscheplanowa alone on an empty stage was overlaid, in my mind's eye, with that of Lars Eidinger's Hamlet, in the opening scene of Ostermeier's *Hamlet*, in the rain with Claudius, Gertrude and Polonius under umbrellas beside him, while the gravedigger, in a slapstick routine that becomes wilder and wilder, wrestles with the coffin (Figure 3). Regardless of whether or not Ostermeier's directorial vision for this scene was influenced by a prior acquaintance with Heiner Müller's adaptation, or even with Gotscheff's stage production of it in 2007, the process of watching the two productions in lockdown tangled those two threads at that moment. It catalysed a dense and significant connection that momentarily conferred on the Gertrude/Ophelia of Ostermeier's production the breast cancer of *Hamletmaschine*'s Madonna.

As a consequence of this anachronic meshing together of multiple productions that began to connect them in unforeseen ways, the intermingling in Ostermeier's *Hamlet* of the characters of Gertrude and Ophelia, performed by Judith Rosmair in the Avignon broadcast, acted as a portal of sorts into multiple other productions of *Hamlet*. Rosmair's Gertrude morphed into Ophelia by growling into a microphone and distorting her face into a silent scream while removing her sunglasses and wig. At the point of transition, her wide-open mouth issuing a silent primal scream began to ricochet through this and all other *Hamlet* broadcasts I was watching at the time. The theatregram of a woman's mouth distorted into a silent scream distilled Shakespeare's play, and specifically the female figures within it (not just Ophelia and Gertrude, but also Hamlet whenever he was performed by a woman, as he often was) into the ultimate expression of the inability to articulate one's distress.

Figure 3 Old Hamlet's burial in Thomas Ostermeier, dir. *Hamlet*. photo arno declair, berlin.

The primal silent scream surfaced, potently, in the second act of the version of *Hamlet* directed for The Wooster Group by Liz LeCompte,[9] where it functioned as a means of tying multiple *Hamlet*s together in a dense concentration of intertextual hauntings. That production itself, as Jennifer Parker-Starbuck points out, created an analogy between the way 'Hamlet confronts the ghost of his father' and how the production 'confronts the ghost of another *Hamlet*', namely the Broadway production starring Richard Burton and directed by John Gielgud recorded in 1964 (2009, p. 23). Throughout LeCompte's *Hamlet*, the digitally modified version of the Gielgud-Burton *Hamlet* was projected onto a large screen at the rear of the stage and meticulously re-enacted by The Wooster Group's actors.

---

[9] *Hamlet* was among half a dozen streams shared by The Wooster Group, including *To You, the Birdie! (Phèdre)*, *Rumstick Road* and *House/Lights*.

Arguably, the Gielgud-Burton *Hamlet* is itself haunted by a host of earlier *Hamlet*s: those of Gielgud himself, which he performed between 1929 and 1946 but never recorded for the screen. In the Gielgud-Burton *Hamlet*, Gielgud's pedigree as Hamlet is incorporated through his performance of Old Hamlet's Ghost as voice without a body asking to be remembered. The Wooster Group initially suppressed Gielgud's ghostly presence by having Ari Fliakos dub the voice-over from the wings (something that is not visible in the broadcast; Worthen, 2010, p. 134) but then went on to self-consciously reinforce that internal haunting in the already profoundly metatheatrical scene of the players' arrival in Elsinore.

At that point in The Wooster Group's staging, the Gielgud-Burton film stopped playing in the background, prompting Scott Shepherd's Hamlet to pull a video of Kenneth Branagh's 1996 *Hamlet* film instead. With the deliberate interruption of the Gielgud-Burton film focusing attention firmly not on the actors on stage but on the screen behind them, Charlton Heston as Branagh's Player King was first shown speaking with the sound switched off. Shepherd drew attention to the tension between live performance (where things can go wrong) and the infinite replayability of the mediated (where things can evidently also go wrong), and between the eloquent body and the expressive voice, by adjusting the sound and then, with a throwaway 'sorry' to cover up the glitch, replaying the few seconds of film with both Heston's body and voice.

Mesmerised, Shepherd sat watching the recording. For that brief moment, he was a Hamlet who was unmoored from any obvious re-enactment of a prior incarnation of the role and became an original, unique Hamlet, watching the Player King perform, as it were, for the first time, momentarily unhaunted by theatrical ghosts. Then, gingerly, he began to mimic Heston's gestures and succumbed, once more, to this play's and this production's repetition compulsion. With Heston's voice continuing as voice-over, John Gielgud himself now appeared on the screen as the voiceless body of old Priam, stumbling helplessly amid the burning ruins of Troy before succumbing to Pyrrhus' fatal blow. This citation of Gielgud's body in Branagh's *Hamlet*, cited in turn in The Wooster Group's re-performance of the Burton-Gielgud film, tied together the ghosts of Gielgud's unfilmed performances and the screen memories of

Burton and Branagh, propelling them into the space of The Wooster Group's live performance which was itself recorded and digitally broadcast to become yet another *Hamlet* ready for citation and redeployment in ever new contexts.

Thrust, as The Wooster Group's *Hamlet* stream was, into the context of the vortex of pandemic *Hamlet*s in April/May 2020, however, it was not Gielgud's unexpected appearance as Priam which stood out. Instead, it was Judi Dench's equally unexpected appearance as Hecuba that emerged as the main point at which the tangled lines of productions developed on separate continents in 2007 combined into a dense meshwork. Assisted by Shepherd's Hamlet, Kate Valk, the production's Gertrude and Ophelia, did some additional multi-roling work as one of the players and came centre stage to re-mediate Dench's performance. With Dench on the upstage main screen, Valk's face was captured by an on-stage camera in extreme close up and live-streamed on a smaller television screen (Figure 4). At a single glance, you could see three versions of the 'same' gaping mouth in a fixed expression of impotent grief: Dench at the rear, Valk's live-streamed close-up in the middle distance, and Valk's performance in the theatre closest up and smallest. The effect of this *mise-en-abyme* was uncanny: a multiplication of a silent scream that erased the difference between several characters and performers and that, in so doing, powerfully enmeshed The Wooster Group's *Hamlet* in Ostermeier's production with its similar centring of blurred female subjectivities on the painfully gaping mouth of Judith Rosmair's Gertrude morphing into Ophelia.

That multiplication of a silent gaping mouth, in turn, became tightly entangled with Robert Wilson's landmark production of *Hamletmaschine*, which compulsively returned to the image of a dusty female figure seated on a swivel chair who repeatedly contorted her face until, with her mouth gaping wide, she became a fixed, surreal embodiment of distress. Meanwhile, on another part of the stage, three identically dressed and made-up women sitting at a table repeatedly stuffed their entire hands into their mouths to stifle their screams before the camera returned to showing the dusty woman screaming silently from yet another angle in a 'ritual' that was repeated with utmost precision. As Gordon Rogoff saw it, the sequence suggested 'an overwhelming anxiety, frightened Beckettians doing something – anything –

Figure 4 Hamlet (Scott Shepherd) assisting the player (Kate Valk) with Judi Dench on the big screen in The Wooster Group's *Hamlet*, dir. Elizabeth LeCompte. © The Wooster Group/Courtesy The Wooster Group. Screengrab.

while waiting for the next event' (Rogoff, 1986, pp. 55). Seated in my own swivel chair at my desk, the gaping mouths stuffed with fists tied the by now insistently – almost obsessively – recurring motif of the silent scream to the present anguish of lockdown. These helpless, compulsively repeated gestures of fists painfully rammed into open mouths stood in for the individual's inability to speak of private suffering when faced with the knowledge that others who did not have the privilege of staying safe at home were fighting for their lives, fighting for their breaths.

With Wilson's *Hamletmaschine* too unnerving to watch in a single sitting, the suppressed, impotent anguish communicated by these women in his choreography bled seamlessly into Johan Simons' 2020 production of *Hamlet* at the Schauspielhaus Bochum, which incorporated segments of *Hamletmaschine* and which I watched bracketed by segments of Wilson's production. With the two productions side-by-side, it was impossible to ignore the extent to which Simons' incorporation of mime and highly stylised choreography of the play's clowns (messengers, gravediggers, Osric) echoed Wilson's staging if not in a specific detail, then certainly in the overall surrealist aesthetic.

Most of all and predictably by now, they merged into a single scream of enraged impotence and exhaustion in the penultimate beat of Simons' staging on Johannes Schütz' strikingly sparse white set, populated only by a vast metal sheet and a brightly lit hanging globe whose revolutions around the stage signalled the passage of time in a space that never changed and from which there was no escape (Figure 5). Filmed in front of an empty auditorium for inclusion in the virtual Berliner Theatertreffen of 2020 after the live run was interrupted by lockdown, the empty stalls acted as a constant reminder of the rupture caused by the pandemic. At what looked remarkably like a deliberate social distance of 2 m/6 ft, Sandra Hüller's Hamlet and Dominik Dos-Reis's Laertes stood opposite each other for their duel. '*Fang an*' – 'begin', Hamlet resignedly challenged Laertes. '*Fang an*', he just as resignedly answered. More insistently, Hamlet retorted '*Fang an*', and Laertes responded with the same level of challenge, prompting round after round of challenges until the actors were hoarse with screaming '*Fang an!*' at each other, mouths contorted in a rage that was entirely dissociated from any other physical expression of aggression or agency. Exhausted to

Figure 5 Hamlet (Sandra Hüller), set design by Johannes Schütz. *Hamlet*,
dir. Johan Simon, 2020. © JU Bochum.

death from this screaming match which nobody seemed to hear or care
about, each wrapped in their individual grief for the loss of fathers, sister,
lover, friend, they stumbled towards each other and briefly held hands
before continuing towards the edge of the stage where they lay down to die.

No matter that Wilson's choreography dated back to 1986 and that
Simons' production was premiered before an audience weeks before the
reality of the Covid-19 pandemic hit home: the context of viewing infused
these screams with a cumulative force that reverberated between all these
Hamlet productions. Whether silent or voiced unheeded, the screams
seemed to speak specifically to the present of April/May 2020 in which
mouths – open, exhaling, gasping for breath, intubated, covered in masks,
incapable of speech, clasped shut – had become powerful signifiers of

pandemic contagion and pain. The screaming, gaping mouths of all these women in the 2020 *Hamlet* streams were capable of reaching back across the centuries to the cries, groans and kissing mouths of the grieving widows, mothers and orphans of the 1603 plague whom Dekker invokes as his Muses:

> You desolate hand-wringing widowes, that beate your bosomes ouer your departing husbands: you wofully distracted mothers that with disheueled haire falne into swounds, whilst you lye kissing the insensible cold lips of your breathlesse Infants: you out-cast and downe-troden Orphanes, that shall many a yeare hence remember more freshly to mourne, when your mourning garments shall looke olde and be forgotten. . . . *Eccho* forth your grones. (C3 r–C3 v)

In a final act of viral contagion, all these screams in *Hamlet* broadcasts jumped species barriers for me as they morphed into what may be the original silent scream of German theatre: the almost unbearably long, unbearably silent scream Helene Weigel's Mother Courage emits when she fails to save her son from execution in Brecht's own Berliner Ensemble production of *Mutter Courage und ihre Kinder*, recorded in 1957 and streamed, unexpectedly, on 15 May 2020, as I had just got to the end of watching my tenth *Hamlet/Hamletmaschine* broadcast.

What's Mother Courage to me, or I to Mother Courage, that I should weep for her/Gertrude/Ophelia/Laertes/Hamlet and all the bereaved of epidemics past and present?

1.1.2 Playing with the Dead in Dimiter Gotscheff's *Hamletmaschine*

Shakespeare's view is the view of the epoch. . . . The dead have their place on his stage.

(Heiner Müller, 'Shakespeare a Difference', p. 174)

Hamlet's Hecuba-question draws attention to theatre's ability to make us grieve for the dead of the past, to mourn people we have never met. Despite Hamlet's marvel at the absurdity of the Player King's tears, he is compelled to acknowledge the bereavement felt at the loss of a person who, in the moment of theatrical commemoration, is uniquely valued and can be wept for more cathartically than Hamlet, in his private grief, can weep for his own father. In *The Mousetrap* that follows, Hamlet again experiments with theatre as a social ritual of commemoration: the play that is designed to 'catch the conscience of a King' (2.2.524) is also a means of making his father come back to life, not once, but twice: first in the dumb show in which he is killed, and second in the play for which he rises again to be killed once more. That play, in turn, prompts the father's ghost to reappear again to admonish Hamlet one more time in what the first Quarto stage direction '*in his nightgown*' suggests is an impromptu private appearance in Gertrude's chamber: 'Do not forget' (Q1,11.58; 3.4.109). More than the play's inadequate funerals, which in the repurposing of 'baked meats' for the widow's 'marriage tables' and their 'maimed rites' appear to serve the purpose of forgetting rather than remembering (1.2.180–1; 5.1.198), it is theatre and storytelling that allow effective mourning to take place.

Running counter to the individuation of remembrance the play repeatedly foregrounds, the 'mingle-mangle' of lockdown *Hamlet* streams that was capable of conflating screams past and present into a seemingly universal expression of human distress stripped the Shakespearean text of its eloquence and his characters of their individuality. In a phase of the pandemic when the extent to which Covid-19 discriminates between socio-economic and ethnic groups and exacerbates pre-existing inequalities was only beginning to become apparent, the manner in which the virus seemed indiscriminate in its attack on older people resonated with early modern accounts of the plague. René Girard expounds how the plague's distinctiveness 'is that it ultimately destroys all forms of distinctiveness. The plague overcomes all obstacles, disregards all frontiers. All life, finally, is turned into death, which is the supreme undifferentiation' (1974, p. 834). In April 2020, news reports of refrigerated trucks and mass burials in New York and of temporary morgues in Kent and Gloucestershire presented death as a logistical challenge. The evening news broadcasts went through their grim ritual of counting the number of contagions, hospital admissions and deaths and showing graphs that expressed individual human destinies as a 'curve' that needed 'flattening'. Meanwhile the bereaved, regardless of the cause of death, had to adjust to the maimed rites of live streams of socially distanced funerals with no more than six mourners, Zoom memorial services and deferred burials of ashes.

Against this backdrop, the injunction by Old Hamlet's Ghost to remember him and Hamlet's matching request, in the midst of the carnage of Act 5, that his own story be told struck a particularly strong chord in their insistence on the value of their individual lives and on the need for continued memorialisation. It is in this context that a live-streamed performance of Heiner Müller's *Die Hamletmaschine* stood out for the poignancy with which it performed a maimed rite of individual memorialisation that defied any attempt to subsume a human life into a statistic. Against all the odds, two actors brought a dead player back to strut and fret upon the stage of an eerily empty theatre once more to play with them, with the aim of remembering him and, through him, mourn the loss of theatre as a communal activity of bodily co-presence.

Heiner Müller is known for his suspicion of facile attempts to read what he called a *fatale Aktualität* or 'fatal topicality' into productions of his plays: David Barnett explains how the playwright was keen 'to limit facile connections between text and context' (Barnett 2014, p. 188). Such a connection between text and context, however, became unavoidable when, on 26 April 2020, the Deutsches Theater Berlin invited viewers to its live stream of a revival of Bulgarian actor-director Dimiter Gotscheff's production of Müller's *Hamletmaschine*.

As Gotscheff's conceived it in 2007, his *Hamletmaschine* was performed on a bare black stage with ten rectangular grave openings that always threatened to engulf the performers. By reconceiving Müller's play as a monologue that could be segmented, repeated, and shared between himself and his fellow actors, with the roles of Hamlet and Ophelia distributed across several bodies, Gotscheff uncoupled Müller's text from affect and subjectivity. The result was a staging of the text that constantly challenged the naturalist theatre's fundamental investment in the connection between text, body and emotion. Where in Wilson's 1986 production of *Hamletmaschine*, repetitions had an unsettling identicality in the precision of their choreography, in Gotscheff's interpretation of the play, repetitions enabled the performers to try out various modes of delivery, from catatonic to quietly charged to yelling at the top of their voices. Each mode of delivery destabilised the viewer's understanding of the relationship between the speaker and the words yet further and undermined any easy attribution of 'authenticity' to the emotions on such transparently performative display.

When the production was invited to tour to Havana for a guest performance in the autumn of 2013, Gotscheff was within only a few weeks of his death and too ill to travel. He therefore had his own performance recorded to enable his young fellow performers, Alexander Khuon and Valery Tscheplanowa, to perform in Havana alongside the film in a manner that embedded his physical absence but virtual presence in the production in a further dislocation of body from text and live affect.[10]

Every year since then, the Deutsches Theater Berlin has, on Gotscheff's birthday on 26 April, re-staged this production with live performances by Khuon and Tscheplanowa alongside Gotscheff's recorded performance as part of its Kammerspiele repertoire. Billed as a 'premiere' and a 'special' event in the theatre's programme of archival broadcasts, the live stream on 26 April 2020 *zum Gedenken an Dimiter Gotscheff* / 'in memory of Dimiter Gotscheff' therefore constituted a unique recasting of this yearly commemorative theatrical event. The live surviving actors performed a private theatrical revival of and with Gotscheff that repeatedly crossed the boundaries between the living and the dead, even as the alternation between live and recorded performances made the stage itself oscillate between featuring the open graves of the 2013 set and the uninterrupted black boards that supported the bodies of Khuon and Tscheplanowa.

The broadcast opened with a shot of the inside of the locked-down theatre, whose empty auditorium was shrouded in funereal black dustsheets that recalled the black hangings in which early modern theatres were decked for performances of tragedies. Amid the dustsheets, three camera operators at an emphatic social distance from one another directed their cameras towards the empty stage, whose black boards bore the scuffs of a multitude of performances in better times. At opposite ends of the front row, Khuon

---

[10] Information available on www.deutschestheater.de/programm/archiv/a-e/hamletmaschine/.

and Tscheplanowa sat looking blankly at the empty stage while on the soundtrack, the animated buzz of the absent audience ghosted the presence of the broadcast's remote viewer. If, in Wilson's *Hamletmaschine*, Beckettian waiting had been the catalyst for apparently unmotivated constant busyness, here, the performers seemed to be in a Pyrrhus-like suspension of time that was entirely in tune with public health stay-at-home messaging as they 'Did nothing' (*Hamlet*, 2.2.404). For a long time.

Then, finally, they got up and walked onto the stage, two metres apart, looked at each other, and walked off into opposite aisles, with the empty stage now emphasising the gulf that separated them from each other as well as from us. Khuon re-entered and, as the uncanny canned audience hum subsided, addressed a dialogue between two bankers taken from Müller's dramatic poem 'Mommsen's Block' directly to the absent audience from downstage centre. As his own voice echoed on the theatre's sound system, he repeated what he had said just a few moments earlier, with a second echo gradually blending in another part of his soliloquy – a haunting of the actor by himself that he sometimes paused to listen to, alone with his divided self, before finishing with the instruction: *Arbeiten. Und nicht verzweifeln* – 'Work. And don't despair'. Over the now empty stage, his voice continued to reverberate, bouncing off the emptiness. Work. And don't despair. Work. And don't despair. Work . . .

Thereafter, Gotscheff's performance of *Hamletmaschine* took over, in accented German with occasional lapses into Gotscheff's native Bulgarian. This intense, reflective solo performance on a grave-strewn set with its occasional acknowledgement of the laughter of Gotscheff's live audience on the recording was intercut, after the end of the first text fragment of *Hamletmaschine*, with Tscheplanowa's live re-performance, alone in the present, of that same text as a rapid scream-like expression of rage pressed out of her in a single push. A second push jumped to Müller's third extract, set in the University of the Dead. Exhausted and quiet, Tscheplanowa then reverted to the second extract, Ophelia's devastating account of her attempted suicides. She walked off and Gotscheff reappeared to haltingly re-perform Ophelia's speech, shuffling around the stage like a lost soul, both long gone and yet still here, no more nor less virtual on our screens than 'live' Tscheplanowa.

The live stream thus movingly revived Gotscheff's performance and let him play on the stage of the Deutsches Theater once more, supported by actors whose 'flesh memory' of their own prior performances with him, to invoke Rebecca Schneider's term, had, through the repetition of 'a ritual act', enabled his performance to remain (2001, p. 105). By framing the recording of Gotscheff's performance with their own vital, vibrant presence, Khuon and Tscheplanova infused it with life even as the recording of Gotscheff blended in with the live stream of Khuon's and Tscheplanova's own performances to 'flatten' all of them together into the rigid two dimensionality of the broadcast. Put differently, while the living actors seemed able, for the duration of the ritual, to pull Gotscheff back into the space of the theatre as if in a séance, the medium of the broadcast juxtaposed their liveness with his recordedness in such a manner as to make them all feel equally alive and dead, present and absent.

In the end, however, the performance brought home the ultimate impossibility to remain when, in Gertrude's trite phrase, 'all that lives must die' (1.2.72). After Gotscheff's final scene, Khuon reappeared to address two extracts of poems by Heiner Müller to the camera in the empty auditorium, breaking through the fourth wall of the broadcast to address each of us directly in our separate homes. The first of these, 'The Hyena', is a meditation on the inevitability of the eventual disappearance even of the steel of tanks marooned in the desert. The hour of the hyena, Müller suggests, will have come when no trace is left of human beings, whose strongest material defences against death and forgetfulness must eventually corrode.

The second extract was taken from Müller's response to Conrad's *Heart of Darkness* and spoke directly to the frustrations of lockdown with a fantasy about travel to Malaysia, Thailand, Korea and Yemen, jolting the viewer back into the more trivial concerns of the present. That final bit said, Khuon took off his head mic and walked off the stage into the auditorium. After a pause, Tscheplanowa, now barefoot and vulnerable, with her eyes fixed on the camera, walked to the centre of the stage. There, as the Ophelia/Electra of the final fragment of *Hamletmaschine*, she launched into the disconcertingly serene promise: '*Ich ersticke die Welt, die ich geboren habe, zwischen meinen Schenkeln. . . . Es lebe der Haß, die Verachtung, der Aufstand, der Tod*'

(Müller, 2001a, p. 554) – 'I will suffocate the world which I gave birth to, between my thighs. . . . Long live hate, loathing, rebellion, death' (Müller, 2001b, p. 8). Stepping yet closer to make eye contact with the viewer, she abruptly tilted her head back for a harrowing silent scream (more harrowing for being silent and profoundly enmeshed with all the other silent screams) before she, too, walked out of shot into the stalls.

As the screen went black, applause rang out over the empty auditorium and the lights came back on to show the younger Tscheplanowa and Khuon hand-in-hand with Gotscheff, taking a curtain call. Past and present performers were co-present in a theatrical environment that was both intensely 'live' in its undeniable pandemic setting and yet unreachably remote and 'dead' in its recorded stream. I could hear the disembodied past audience applauding as I found myself unable to clap along, sitting still at my desk, socially distanced, both here and yet also uncannily there, in the empty theatre. Still ringing in my ears with a force that punched right through from Gotscheff's life to mine was the following segment of text which Gotscheff, foaming at the mouth, had repeated with increasingly desperate and incoherent obsession in his final speech:

> *Mein Drama hat nicht stattgefunden. Das Textbuch ist verlor-*
> *engegangen. Die Schauspieler haben ihre Gesichter an den*
> *Nagel in der Garderobe gehängt. In seinem Kasten verfault*
> *der Souffleur. Die ausgestopften Pestleichen im*
> *Zuschauerraum bewegen keine Hand. Ich gehe nach Hause*
> *und schlage die Zeit tot, einig / mit meinem ungeteilten*
> *Selbst. . . . Ich will nicht mehr sterben. Ich will nicht mehr*
> *töten.* (Müller, 2001a, pp. 551–2).

> My drama has not taken place. The script has been lost.
> The actors have hung their faces on the dressing room's
> pegs. The prompter rots in his box. The stuffed plague-
> corpses in the audience don't move a finger. I go home and
> kill time, at one / with my undivided self. . . . I don't want
> to die any more. I don't want to kill any more. (my
> translation)

The audience imagined here are the corpses of plague victims, but the very nihilistic despair of Müller's texts, spoken by a dead performer with such urgent appeal to the present in his desire not to die and kill, acted as a bridge between my present and Gotscheff's, in a faraway theatre of the past. In reaching back to Gotscheff across the abyss of death, in acknowledging the distance separating them from their audience through their direct address to the empty auditorium, Khuon and Tscheplanowa also performed theatre as a ritual séance capable of bridging impossible divides, bringing the living and the dead, the present and the absent, together for a fleeting moment. Despite the production's ostensible denial of individual characterisation, subjectivity and the affect that connects the text with the performer's body in naturalist theatre, this revival-as-memorial service ended up resisting the undifferentiation of the plague and instead celebrating the distinctiveness of a performer who had asserted his ability to be 'at one/with my undivided self'.

1.2 'You speak a language that I understand not': Watching Ivo van Hove's Het Temmen van de Feeks

Emboldened by the ease with which I was suddenly able to access European Shakespeare productions, and invigorated by the brilliance of the work I was watching, I spent much of April 2020 trawling the Internet to find as many of these productions as I could. While *Hamlet* was the play that appeared in the greatest variety of versions, from puppet play (Hidden Theatre's *Fratricide Punished*) to avant-garde adaptation (the two *Hamletmaschine* productions and The Wooster Group's *Hamlet*), three German versions (Ostermeier, Simons and Weise), an opera (Thomas' *Hamlet* from the New York Metropolitan Opera) and mainstream performances (the most recent productions by the RSC and Shakespeare's Globe), other plays were far less frequently streamed, with many only available in a single version. The overfamiliarity of *Hamlet*, therefore, and the languages within which *Hamlet* was performed (English, German, French – my three main languages), stood in stark contrast to some of the plays that were rarer and performed in languages I could not understand and had to access via subtitles.

Macbeth, for example, was a play I only saw in subtitled Polish. Through the kind of meshing which I have argued was a characteristic effect of binge watching in lockdown, Grzegorz Jarzyna's Polish *2007: Macbeth* (2005) became deeply entangled with the stream of Katie Mitchell's *Orlando* (2019) from the Berliner Schaubühne on the one hand, and with Christian Weise's graphic novel–inspired *Hamlet* stream from the Gorki Theater Berlin (2020) on the other. What connected these productions was the manner in which the construction of character intersected with a split-screen aesthetic that forced the viewer in the theatre no less than the viewer of the archival recordings to choose which part of these productions' rigorously zoned sets to concentrate on. This, in turn, demanded that the viewer become involved in the construction of character and narrative. Much like the reader of the graphic novels the Gorki *Hamlet* so obviously referenced, that is, we were asked to read the contents of a single frame while also juggling the montage-like information conveyed by the spatial relationships of frames in relation to one another (Bizzocchi, 2009).

Within this meshwork of streams, Jarzyna's Iraq War–inspired *2007: Macbeth* stood out for the optical trick it played on its remote viewers. Viewers in the disused Waryński Factory (Warsaw), where the show was filmed in 2006, were from the start of the production facing the enormous cavernous stage. Subdivided into a hangar-like space on one side, a creepy narrow corridor going from the front of the stage to its rear in the middle, and a domestic interior with an upstairs area and separate backstage prayer room visible through an open door on the opposite side, the size of the stage allowed several scenes to sometimes be performed concurrently, so that theatre audiences had to decide where to look from the start of the play.

In the archival broadcast, however, the spatial relationship between these zones was entirely obscured during the first half of the tragedy, lulling the viewer into a mode of viewing that was 'immersive' and 'natural' in the manner of the invisible editing familiar from the naturalistic aesthetic of mainstream cinema and television. In effect, for half of the stream, the stage acted as a film set, with edits switching between spaces and plotlines as if they were worlds apart from one another, while shots of actors co-present in a single space followed the rules of continuity editing and placed the broadcast viewer within the set. For viewers of the stream, therefore, it was impossible to understand how the different spaces functioned theatrically, as part of a single stage set viewed by spectators from the vantage point of the stalls.

It was only as the world and mental health of the Macbeths fractured that the camera retreated and began to show the entire stage. Now only was filmic naturalism (and the 'natural order') revealed as an illusion. With the actors reduced to tiny figures within the enormous set, broadcast viewers were abruptly given the responsibility for deciding where to look and were asked to change from a filmic to a theatrical understanding of both space and characters. As the complexity of the viewing experience, the stress levels of the tragedy and the protagonists' trauma in this relentlessly bleak production increased, the subtitles became ever more important to orient the foreign-language viewer within the set and the action without adding an extra level of difficulty of access.

The split stage of *2007: Macbeth* and the way in which its remediation in the broadcast mirrored the thematic fracturing of the natural order and protagonists' minds within the play made it mesh with another 'foreign-language' broadcast: Internationaal Theater Amsterdam's production of *Het Temmen van de Feeks / The Taming of the Shrew*.[11] To my knowledge, this was the only archival stream of this play broadcast during the first lockdown. I had recently written about Ivo van Hove's extraordinary conflation of *Coriolanus*, *Julius Caesar* and *Antony and Cleopatra* into *Roman Tragedies*, which I saw as a durational performance when Internationaal Theater Amsterdam toured to London in 2017, and I was determined to watch whatever else I could by that company. The hitch was that this production was not subtitled and that my Dutch is limited to what I can puzzle out using a combination of English, Swiss German and Standard German. As a result, this turned out to be my most challenging and concerted effort in intercultural engagement during lockdown.

As I sat down to watch the show, I knew that this would be a solo adventure without the 'event-connectedness' that had grouped me together with other viewers into a virtual community for most other productions

---

[11] The stream, at the time of going to press, remains online at https://ita.nl/nl/episodes/het-temmen-van-de-feeks/824714/.

(Allred, 2022, forthcoming). I therefore switched gears and went from binge watching as many different productions as possible to repeatedly watching this single broadcast, replacing the 'noise' generated by too many versions of the same thing with the very different 'noise' of dealing with a language for which I had no competence. During the seemingly endless, sunny, house-and-garden-bound days of May and June 2020, I went back over segments I did not understand, with the Norton anthology on my desk, googling words and asking a Dutch colleague for help with translations and local knowledge. The affordances of an online stream combined with the expansion of time as lockdown spring turned into lockdown summer made this unlike any ordinary theatrical encounter with Shakespeare in a foreign language. Normally, you might sit in a theatre abroad, in an uninterruptible performance, feeling the play as much through the responses of the native speakers around you as you do through your prior knowledge of the plot. Normally, you might allow yourself to not understand and embrace the ephemerality of theatre.

But these were not normal times. The experience of watching *Het Temmen* was effectively the reverse of the shot of adrenaline and intense concentration of watching Ostermeier's *Hamlet*: it was a single-minded and prolonged effort to make sense of this bewildering production in which so many actions – from refrigerator sex to urine drinking and bare-breasted pizza regurgitation – took the play in startling new directions.

The impasse only resolved itself when I began to accept my linguistic incompetence not as an obstacle but as an invitation to focus on the signifying power of actions and sound (as opposed to language). After all, when Hamlet complains that 'groundlings' are 'capable of nothing but inexplicable dumb shows and noise' (3.2.10–11), he is acknowledging their competence in understanding theatrical performances in a visceral manner that does not depend on literary and linguistic competence. Surely, I was not any less competent than Hamlet's groundlings (who were, William West reminds us, more commonly referred to as *understanders*, suggesting they were actually not quite as uncomprehending as Hamlet suggests (2006, p. 114)).

My 'understanding' of this production will inevitably be very different from that of a Dutch speaker – but are there advantages to not understanding the words? Are there things I saw and heard that became salient *because* I don't speak Dutch?

Noise is the dominant note of the first part of this production and broadcast, both aurally and visually. On stage, noise is metaphorically created both by the setting amid the chaos of carnival, with an initially tidy stage gradually overwhelmed by mess and dirt, and by the juxtaposition of separate performance spaces that is similar to that of *2007: Macbeth*. There is a flexible forestage space, which functions as a street in Padua, the inside of Baptista's and later Petruchio's houses, and the road between Padua and Verona. There is also a large room in a glass box behind, which is a private space inhabited by the women of the play and their suitors. The action continuously plays in both those spaces at once, creating an overload of visual information much in the manner of Jarzyna's *2007: Macbeth*. However, whereas in the second half of the *2007: Macbeth* broadcast, a split screen aesthetic is created simply by virtue of letting the camera retreat to the back of the auditorium and reveal the full width of the stage, in Peter de Baan and Floor Maas' video work for *Het Temmen*, the screen itself is split into two, three and sometimes four video feeds that are juxtaposed into what amounts to a visual assault (Figures 6 and 7).

The noise is also aural, with the carnival setting repeatedly leading to eruptions of rowdiness from the suitors and their male servants, who roar nationalistic and xenophobic football chants, get drunk and bully any stranger who has the misfortune of wanting to join the queue of suitors for Bianca's hand. At one point, our attention is split between Katherina in the background mummifying Bianca head-to-toe in black latex in revenge for Bianca writing *"KAATJE KUTHOER"*/"KATIE CUNTWHORE" across Katherina's window, while in the foreground, the rival suitors subject Tranio to a shower of spit (deeply uncomfortable to watch in a pandemic) and then force him to kiss Petruchio's exposed backside.

I daresay that even for Dutch viewers, this is a loud production – the colleague I asked for help described one 'song' as 'Fascist, populist, nationalist, mixed with superficial, offensive student and football chanting' and another as 'a mish-mash of partly unintelligible shouting mixed with fragments of easily recognizable soundbites from Dutch songs and, in particular, football-related elements.' However, what was occasional

Figures 6, 7, 8 Visual and aural noise for the wedding of Katharina (Halina Reijn). *Het Temmen van de Feeks*, dir. Ivo van Hove, 2009. © Internationaal Theater Amsterdam

incomprehension for him was totally overwhelming for me: a wall of noise – howls, shouting, chanting, slamming doors, stamping of feet and drumming – that was close to unbearable.

The aural assault came to a head a first time in Petruchio's and Katharina's first encounter, a shouting match that culminated with

Figures 6, 7, 8 (Cont.)

Katherina seeking refuge inside a fridge. Having first lain down on the fridge to perform imaginary clitoral stimulation on its base, Petruchio repeatedly kicked its door until Katherina tumbled out of it, visibly shaken. Aural violence against Katherina combined here for the first time with the suggestion of a sexual practice that connected a focus specifically on Katherina's implied sexual pleasure with her physical and aural subjugation.

The noise mounted to a second climax as Katherina was waiting for Petruchio to arrive for their wedding. That is when the assembled men, in a mix of football and carnival outfits, started to chant and stamp, exacerbating her isolation and humiliation, alone in her wedding dress. This sequence was one of several examples where the split-screen technique of the broadcast worked, at first, to complement the aural noise with a crescendo of visual noise. Katherina was first shown defensively holding her ears in a close-up on the top right corner of the tripartite screen (Figure 6), which then split into four segments with two diagonally arranged separate shots of beleaguered Katherina (Figure 7), until the image resolved itself in the relative quiet of Katherina alone, still holding her ears to fight off the din (Figure 8). The sequence, as it were, pulled the viewer into Katherina's headspace and away from her tormentors, with the splitting of the screen used not so much to represent the simultaneous action occurring on different parts of the stage, as interpretively to focus on Katherina as the affective anchor of the scene.

After the wedding, Katherina attempted to turn the tables on Petruchio by assuming the lead in a chant with the mob of men as she refused to follow Petruchio back to Verona. But that rebellion was short lived: it ended with her being outclamoured by Petruchio, who roared and stamped her into submission. And then, in Petruchio's house, Katherina was subjected to a din of carnival pipes and drums, kept awake by being shaken by Grumio to the sound of loud music.

In other words, as the production wore on, as someone who could hear more sound than meaning, more noise than words, I felt myself increasingly put in a position analogous to that of Katherina: pummelled into submission by the sensory overload and desperate for a moment of respite, of calm, of clarity.

A few years ago, Sally Templeman pointed out that some of the earliest performances of *The Taming of the Shrew* took place in inn-yard playhouses. She argued that at the height of the taming plot, playgoers would start to smell the tantalising aroma of roast meat wafting into the performance space of the inn-yard from the inn's kitchens just as Petruchio denies Katherina the supposedly burned beef. As Templeman explains, this was likely to have triggered a mode of somatic and affective empathy in the viewers, as '[s]educed by the inn's smells-cape, an onstage-offstage desire for food may have nudged playgoers' sympathy away from Petruccio the shrew tamer, and towards the hungry shrew' (2013, p. 87).

It is an aural version of this somatic empathy with Katherina that my linguistic incompetence exacerbated in this production. Katherina's trademark gesture of cowering and covering her ears was matched by my equivalent desire to shield myself from the assault: I constantly had to force myself to resist the urge to just watch the production on mute.

It all came to a head in the extraordinary scene in which, having been starved, deprived of sleep and then denied the clothes she wanted, loud drumming accompanied the moment when Katherina, standing on a table, lost control of her bladder in front of the tailor and Grumio, while in the glass box behind her Bianca was readied for her wedding. As 'Oh baby,

I love you' started on the soundtrack, triggering a shock of linguistic relief at understanding the English lyrics,[12] Petruchio gently lifted Katherina off the table and then sucked the liquid off the table before looking up at her shocked face with an expression of tenderness and love.

Discussing the scene with Ruth Wilson, Halina Reijn recalls feeling humiliated in the rehearsal room, and recounts how 'That moment marked a turning point' for the character:

> She is at the lowest point of her journey through the play, but by coming up with the suggestion that Hans [Kesting] should lick the water [fake urine], Ivo [van Hove] and Jan [Versweyveld] make it clear that Petruchio is now surrendering to her. They read the play as being about two people, who have absorbed the brutal qualities of the world they live in, and reach out to each other through brutal power play.
>
> (2018, pp. 37–8)

Ivo van Hove puts this more starkly as a falling in love 'between an executioner and his victim, between master and servant, a love that breaks all boundaries'. Blaming the victim in a manner I find unacceptable, he proceeds: 'She kindles the executioner in him and he hurts her body. . . . By breaking everything, something new is created: a relationship between equals' (van Hove, 2018, p. 47). What I saw in this moment was that her humiliation was met by his own abjection, and her shocked recognition of the price of love paved the way for a mutual understanding that was profoundly unsettling as Katherina tentatively felt her way towards accepting the sadomasochistic terms of engagement in this *Fifty Shakespeares of Grey* version of the play.

Having affectively partaken in Katherina's torture by noise, the scene brought me unexpected relief and release and affectively aligned me with her as, in the ensuing sun-and-moon scene, she exhaustedly sat with Petruchio to work out what exactly these terms of engagement might involve.

[12] Song not credited in the broadcast.

As it turned out, they involved breaking theatrical conventions and not just sexual ones, as Hans Kesting dropped the role of Petruchio to heckle a supposedly disruptive member of the audience in the stalls and asked Halina Reijn to join him in this as both herself and Katherina. Kesting sharply turned to the camera and waved at the broadcast audience and, then, with a hand gesture that made his '*zitten blijf*' intelligible even to me, advised broadcast viewers to 'remain seated, as it isn't over yet'. Following an exchange of glances with the other cast members who looked on aghast, Reijn obliged, apologetically at first. When Kesting invited her to do it properly, as his shrew, she threw herself into the heckling with incredulous exhilaration.

As Reijn's Katherina gradually embraced the pleasure of being able to participate in Petruchio's game and understand its rules, I was hit with equivalent pleasure at having understood a significant part of what was going on, including the crucial word '*feeks*' / 'shrew'. My little success in the struggle to overcome the language barrier and be let into the play coincided with the breaking of the theatrical barrier separating character from actor and stage from the audience.

Having struggled up this mountain, I found the remainder of the performance much easier, as the poles were reversed and Petruchio and Katherina represented order and harmony, sitting together quietly in a corner to watch the grotesque disorder, drunkenness and casual sexual aggression of Bianca's wedding party. In sharp contrast with the aural assault of the first half of the production, this final part was almost somnolent in mood and sound. A slow piano soundtrack underscored the laborious, slightly slurred, diction, which made it much easier for me to get my bearings in the dialogue. Even the set design and broadcast style calmed down, with blinds shuttering off the distractions of the glass-walled room at the rear of the stage, and a less hectic editing style with single rather than split screens that helped focus and comprehension.

It was as if a door into the play had been opened. The conclusion, accordingly, made emotional sense and involved Katherina and Petruchio once more breaking through the theatrical fourth wall as, with a tear trickling down her cheek, she addressed her final speech from downstage centre to Petruchio sitting in the stalls before reaching out to him to invite

Figures 9, 10 Petruchio (Hans Kesting) in the audience, listening to Katherina (Halina Reijn) deliver her final speech from the stage. *Het Temmen van de Feeks*, dir. Ivo van Hove, 2009. © Internationaal Theater Amsterdam.

him into an embrace. As the edit switched from Katherina on the stage to Petruchio in the stalls, furthermore, the choice to show both faces in profile on the right of the screen looking out towards the left made of the final speech not so much a confrontation as a common endeavour. The two characters, while opposed, were also ultimately occupying the same position (Figures 9 and 10).

It is hard to know to what extent my reading of this production will ever be 'right' and correspond to that of a native speaker – trawling through the online reviews I am surprised that none of them mentions the production's soundscape and the shift of noise to relative silence that accompanies the pivot in Petruchio and Katherina's relationship. Of course, Ric Knowles is right in warning that taking a work out of 'the cultural context through which it has been produced and has produced its meanings' in this way entails the 'dangers of displacement and loss of cultural specificity' (2004, p. 89). Obviously, too, there is a risk involved in departing from the norms of academic writing about theatre work, which is based on the writer 'position[ing] themselves as securely belonging to a production's target audience, so fully competent in its codes and its context that if they haven't understood it, nobody will' (Dobson, 2013, p. 190).

What the experience shows, however, is that there is value in tackling productions in languages we don't or barely understand, because it sharpens our awareness of language *as emotional soundscape* rather than meaning. It shifts attention towards dumb shows such as Katherina's shielding of her ears, which disappears completely in the second part of the production and makes way for gestures of reaching and hugging that tell a story of their own. As John Russell Brown put it many years ago, 'A member of an audience, at a loss to understand any of the foreign words spoken, may become a more penetrating *viewer*' (1993, p. 31, emphasis in original). I daresay that we may become more penetrating *listeners*, too.

In this case, not speaking the language seemed to confer on me a special kind of privilege. The linguistic deprivation and assault by noise opened up access to a particular somatic empathy for Katherina that made the pivotal moment of Katherina's humiliation and Petruchio's abjection, if not more palateable, then at least in some strange way a relief that eased the way towards allowing the validity of a resolution which I find intellectually and politically unacceptable. As much as I am repulsed by van Hove's suggestion that Katherina somehow 'kindles the executioner' in Petruchio and therefore, he implies, has it coming to her, my *affective* response to the production's soundscape allowed me to achieve a more intuitive acceptance of its value systems even if those values do not accord with mine.

Erin Sullivan observes that aesthetic 'works are fundamentally partici-patory in their design: they are brought to life not simply by the artist who creates them, but also by the auditor or spectator who receives them' (2018b, pp. 120–1). Watching *Het Temmen van de Feeks* in a lockdown that allowed time to become elastic and facilitated the digital viewing practices of stopping the stream, looping back, taking breaks, googling for information and asking for help made it possible to overcome linguistic barriers and reach some level of understanding. Reaching out despite the difficulty to connect, as Katherina does, and acknowledging that connection is something that needs work and acceptance of limitations, is the precondi-tion for being able to upend Katherina's conclusion and proclaim that straws might just be lances, and weaknesses a strength in intercultural theatre watching. We might find that while we cannot quite share each other's experiences, the effort to participate in a *Zwangsvorstellung* may open up ways of understanding that are perhaps not entirely a delusion.

2 Live Digital Shakespeare

Forasmuch as . . . yt appearethe the infection dothe increase . . . we thinke yt fitt that all manner of concourse and publique meetinges of the people at playes, beare-baitinges, bowlinges and other like assemblyes for sportes be forbidden.

(Privy Council letter to the Lord Mayor and Aldermen of the City of London, January 1593, in Dasent 2009, pp. 30–1).

[E]veryone should avoid gatherings and crowded places, such as pubs, clubs and theatres.

(BBC News, www.bbc.co.uk/news/uk-51917562, 16 March 2020).

The shutdown of theatres to slow the rate of infection posed an existential threat for the industry. In the United Kingdom, the Treasury's main eco-nomic rescue package was the Covid-19 'Job Retention Scheme', which enabled companies to 'furlough' members of staff who had been on their payroll on 19 March on 80 per cent of their pay. Many of the freelancers who make up almost half of the UK's theatre industry were either on a short-term contract that did not meet the conditions or between contracts at that time. The scheme therefore left them without a source of income other than the welfare support provided by 'Universal Credit'.[13]

In the anxious months of the first lockdown, it was hard to see how small- to mid-scale companies could continue to employ freelance actors and backstage staff to produce new shows. When, on 5 July, the Treasury announced a £1.57bn Culture Recovery Fund, it soon became apparent that the terms of the rescue package favoured established building-based larger organisations but had little provision for freelancers and production companies without a theatre building. Rescue packages and policies in the United Kingdom instead differentiated between parts of the economy that were worth saving and parts that were not. The dividing line appeared to be drawn between industries that offer long-term, regular employment and parts of the economy, like the creative industries, that depend on short-term contracts and the availability of a large number of freelancers. The mobility and flexibility of this workforce have made them vulnerable to being ignored by policies that rely on a normative understanding of what constitutes 'employment' and a livelihood worth protecting.[14]

For the companies the Culture Recovery Fund did not support, the problem was greatly exacerbated by the torrent of archival broadcasts I discussed in Section 1 of this Element. Because these broadcasts were made available for free, with income generated through donations, audiences rapidly became accustomed to expecting all creative digital content to be if not entirely free of charge, then certainly significantly cheaper than in-person theatre. Spectators who had previously been willing to pay not only premium West End theatre ticket prices but additionally used to generate

---

[13] Universal Credit in the United Kingdom combines all welfare benefits into a single payment, which is capped at £13,399.88 per annum for a single person living outside London (see Equity UK for the types of support available for theatre industry professionals during the pandemic, www.equity.org.uk/media/5543/covid-19-financial-support-guide_-v21.pdf).

[14] See also Erin Sullivan's critique of the 'Fatima's next job could be in cyber' media campaign run by the UK government to encourage artists to 'Rethink. Reskill. Reboot' their careers (2022, forthcoming).

very significant 'additional visitor spend' on travel, food, drinks and babysitting began to recalibrate their expenditures (Shellard, 2004, p. 15). Audience members now thought twice about how much to donate to broadcasting theatres, and donation fatigue soon set in. The results of two large-scale UK-wide surveys of cultural organisations and audience members, which were carried out by cultural consultants Indigo in April and May ('After the Interval') and June and July 2020 ('Act 2'), reveal that there was a large audience for digital work in this period. Yet while more than two-thirds of this audience were ready to pay for new work, only 15 per cent of respondents were willing to pay the same ticket price for a digital show as for a live event (Raines, 2020, pp. 15, 17) – and they were even less willing to pay to see an archival broadcast.[15]

At a time when those trends were beginning to take shape, and I was wallowing in archival broadcasts while wondering whether and how the creative staff involved in their recording were being paid for their labour, I happened upon a theatre review that piqued my interest. Miriam Gillinson's (2020) *Guardian* review of Creation Theatre and Big Telly's co-production of *The Tempest*, which was directed by Big Telly's Artistic Director Zoë Seaton, concluded:

> For a production pulled together in just two weeks, there are impressively few technical glitches. . . . The online setting feels like a naturally confined context, and it's the entrapped characters – including Itxaso Moreno's Ariel and PK Taylor's Caliban – that are most memorable. But it's the audience who are the most excited and exciting characters of all. . . . It's such a joy to enjoy the show together. And that feeling of clapping together, while apart, at the end of the show? The stuff that dreams are made on.

I immediately got on the phone to Creation Theatre's box office and begged my way into obtaining a ticket for the afternoon's show. I skimmed the instructions on the emailed 'ticket' with bemusement, sat down at my

---

[15] For more analysis, see Aebischer and Nicholas, 2020a, pp. 27–31.

desk – and was blown away by the energy of the production and the giddy exuberance at being part of a live theatre audience, able to experience new work in the company of strangers who visibly shared my elation.

By the end of that week, many of my regular watch party friends with whom I'd shared my enthusiasm on Twitter had also watched the show, and we had an hour-long Zoom get together to discuss our impressions. *The Tempest* became a surprise international hit which, following word-of-mouth recommendations via social media and reviews in the United Kingdom's *The Guardian* and BBC Radio 4 and New York's *Time Out* and *The New York Times*, enjoyed a run that was extended into May 2020. This extent of critical attention from both sides of the Atlantic for an Oxford-based company stemmed in part from the scarcity of professional work available to review at that point: *The Tempest* was among the very first professional productions during the pandemic to be performed on the commercial Zoom platform. Creation Theatre and Big Telly's work also stood out and still warrants special attention because their zany combination of virtual backgrounds, theatrical trickery and interaction with the audience, underpinned by professional production values with a handmade aesthetic, remained unique even as other companies pivoted to digital theatre making. Notably CtrlAlt_Repeat, the Willow Globe, the Guildford Shakespeare Company, Prague Shakespeare Company and Shakespeare Happy Hours all started to produce rehearsed readings and professional performances of Shakespeare plays, while Rob Myles and Sarah Peachey created the Zoom-specific The Show Must Go Online (TSMGO), which garnered a significant fan and contributor base, with 'the aim of performing the entire First Folio in the order they are thought to have been written' (Allred and Broadribb, 2022b, forthcoming).[16]

Fired up by the realisation that *The Tempest* had modelled a way for theatre companies to continue to produce new work and pay their free-lancers, from July to October 2020 I teamed up with audience researcher Rachael Nicholas to examine how the company had so successfully adopted digital practices and talk to audience members to guage the potential of digital theatre to endure beyond the pandemic. Much of my summer of

---

[16] Allred and Broadribb (2022b, forthcoming) is the starting point for further research into this lockdown medium.

2020, therefore, was spent talking to Creation Theatre's creatives and production company staff, who had thrown open the virtual doors to the company for us, and immersing myself in their work and that of Big Telly.

Meanwhile, the two companies continued to learn about the affordances and opportunities opened up by the Zoom videoconferencing platform through a programme of work that included a remarkable amount of early modern material. After their joint *Tempest*, Creation Theatre staged a rehearsed reading of *Henry VIII* in June 2020 and went on to host two light-hearted spin-off Shakespeare adaptations by freelancers that included *The Merry Wives of WhatsApp* (September/October 2020) and *Horatio! And Hamlet* (September/November 2020). Big Telly produced *Macbeth* in October 2020. By March 2021, when Creation Theatre produced its *The Duchess of Malfi*, the company, which now had a repertory company of six actors, had made such big strides in its use of technology that, as Amy Borzuk (2021) observed in her review of the production, the Zoom platform was able to 'blend into the production rather than foreground it'.

Putting the technical and industry-focused research that informed our *Digital Theatre Transformation* work aside, the second part of this Element consists of a deep dive into the productions of *The Tempest* and *Macbeth*. I am interested in the extraordinary development of the companies' approach to audience participation and characterisation. I furthermore want to explore the spatial dynamics of performing on Zoom and think about how the platform remediates the complex interplay between *locus*, *platea* and the offstage 'obscene'. Moreover, given that the 2020 digital *Tempest* originated in a 2019 analogue production, is it fair to suggest that the digital version of the production to some extent provides an archival recording of its analogue predecessor? How did the companies adapt their site-specific practices to make them platform-specific? To what extent does the medium of a videoconferencing platform facilitate the remediation of early modern spatial dramaturgies and audience participation and deal with the vexed questions of co-presence and liveness when performers and audiences are all geographically dispersed? What are the limits and dangers of the medium, and how did the productions explore and exploit them?

Behind all those questions lurk the different phases of the pandemic, which fundamentally shaped not only the form but also the meanings made available through these contrasting productions of Shakespeare: the first a utopian fantasy of togetherness, the second a dystopian critique of policy failures and the precariousness of freelancers in the theatre industry.

2.1 From Site-Specific to Platform-Specific Immersion: Creation Theatre and Big Telly's Tempest, 2019–2020

2.1.1 What's Past Is Prologue: Creation Theatre's Analogue *Tempest* and Live Facebook Stream (2019)

Between 19 July and 15 August 2019, Osney Mead, a small island on the outskirts of Oxford, played host to Creation Theatre's *The Tempest* as a site-specific, immersive and participatory production. In an interview at the time, Simon Spencer-Hyde, the production's Prospero, spoke of how Seaton had 'edited the script of *The Tempest* . . . to make it flexible, more of a movable feast that we can tweak and move around', in a quest 'to try and empower the audience as much as possible so they make the choices and it's a game for them' (Mitchell, 2019). The theatrical experience accordingly involved what Jeremy Dennis (2019) described as 'Part escape room, part scavenger hunt, part promenade, part urban exploration, where audience, extras and crew twitch between surveillance dystopias, coffee shop dramas and royal intrigues, alliances shifting and sympathies twisting'.

The production moved between twelve locations and involved the audience at every step of the way. The first of the locations was a large hall in a conference venue decked out as the restaurant of a Creation Cruises ship, which carried the audience and the royals accompanying King Alonso of Naples (Al Barclay) from Tunis to Milan. A sudden tempest brought about by the incursion of Ixtaso Moreno's electrifying punk-inspired Ariel caused the ship's crew and royal party to sway and be tossed from side to side to the sound of thunderous crashing, until the Ship Captain (Giles Stoakley) ordered the table-by-table evacuation of the now shipwrecked audience to the pavement outside.

Thereafter, each audience group followed a different trajectory along a three-km-long route through the interiors of the industrial estate on the island (everything from an old-fashioned hop-on-hop-off double-decker bus to a school and a coffee shop) and its surprisingly wild river paths, to encounter characters and piece together the story of Shakespeare's *Tempest*. Audiences were asked to blend in with their surroundings by assuming the shape of trees and objects whenever a zombie (any cyclist using the footpath or road) approached. They were invited to 'hack' into the surveillance apparatus of Spencer-Hyde's Prospero and were sent to find Caliban (PK Taylor). They listened to the disconsolate King of Naples and helped him pull muddy objects out of the river in his search for his drowned son. In a coffee shop, they were able to observe Annabelle Terry's Miranda fall for Ryan Duncan's Ferdinand in a romance that resulted in a stag party. Each location thus represented an episode in the overall plot of *The Tempest*, with audiences becoming part of the storytelling until everyone reunited back in the conference centre to celebrate Ferdinand and Miranda's wedding.

Other than a handful of reviews, only scant archival traces remain of this production despite the company's half-hearted attempt at producing a Facebook live stream of one performance, which follows Lucy Askew and a group of audience members as they work their way through immersive maze of the play in Osney Meade. After just over an hour, the stream breaks off. Another stream on the Creation Theatre Facebook site picks up the thread with fifteen minutes of shaky mobile phone footage. The footage gives a frustratingly incomplete insight into less than half of the most analogue of productions, dependent on physical co-presence and direct interaction of performers and audiences, serendipitous encounters with unsuspecting cyclists and on participants' willingness to walk significant distances.

The Facebook stream offers only the briefest of glimpses of what Dennis saw as the production's stand-out performance:

> As the audience is steadily divided and conquered on the scramble through the scenes, the soft reality of a summer evening becomes augmented and enhanced by irrepressible stories and unsurpressable [sic] spirits, the very best of which is Itxaso Moreno, thrillingly demonic/elfin, exquisitely elusive, the ghost that haunts the production, Ariel.
>
> (2019; Figure 11)

Figure 11 Steward (Simon Castle) and Ariel (Itxaso Moreno). *The Tempest*, dir. Zoë Seaton for Creation Theatre and Big Telly, 2019. Photo © Richard Budd.

The archive associates Moreno with 'bright-eyed energy' (Lafferty, 2019), intense moments of confrontation and surprise, and most of all with the ephemerality of a performance that resists being captured. In her elusiveness, she comes to embody the force of analogue performance as defined by Peggy Phelan as that which 'cannot be saved, recorded, documented'; as that which 'becomes itself through disappearance' (1993, p. 146). None of the archival traces is capable of capturing the full flavour of this performance and of accounting for the impact it had on its analogue audiences in 2019.

2.1.2 Digital Participation: Remediating *Locus* and *Platea* on Zoom

When, at the very start of the first lockdown, the company reunited to revive *The Tempest* on Zoom with just two weeks of rehearsal, the technological challenge was about how to operate a videoconferencing platform which was entirely new to most of the cast and even the stage manager, Sinéad Owens (credited as 'Zoom wizard'). The artistic challenge was how to retain the production's barmy energy and participatory theatricality in the digital medium and keep it live and open to serendipity.

The two challenges turned out to be interrelated. As members of the company played about with the videoconferencing platform, on their own and together, it became clear that many of its affordances could be used to remediate precisely the flexible relationship between performer and audience which is difficult to achieve in multi-camera theatre broadcasts. While such broadcasts find it easy to portray what Robert Weimann terms the *locus* – the fictional 'fourth-wall' space inhabited by performers who are unaware of the presence of an audience – it is more challenging for them to portray the figural position of the *platea*, which is inhabited by performers capable of acknowledging and communicating directly with their audience (1978, pp. 79–80; see also Aebischer, 2020, pp. 12–27). When, in the theatre, performers address the audience directly, as the actors in the 2019 *Tempest* did much of the time, they are able to generate a reciprocal bond with their audience that facilitates what Hans-Thies Lehmann terms 'an *aesthetic of responsibility (or response-ability)*', which 'can move the *mutual implication of actors and spectators in the theatrical production of images* into the centre' (2006, pp. 185–6, emphasis in the original).

When such moments are remediated through a theatre broadcast, however, the *platea* position is commonly 'transformed into camerawork that pull[s] the viewer into the character's consciousness, creating a cinematic equivalent of theatrical intimacy, in which the technological proximity generated by the zoom lens [stands] in for direct eye contact' (Aebischer, 2020, p. 175). Virtual *platea* spaces are sometimes opened up by companies reaching out to their remote audiences through interactions on other digital platforms, most commonly by inviting their audiences to interact using a shared hashtag on Twitter or joining a YouTube, Instagram or Facebook chat. Crucially, however, while such interactions impact the viewer's *experience* of the performance, save for very few exceptions they have no influence on its shape and on the performers themselves in the moment of the performance. Theatre broadcasts, therefore, do not treat their remote viewers as co-creators, and they substitute technological proximity to a character 'for the response-ability/responsibility, potential dialogue and ethical engagement that are an affordance of direct address in the theatre' (Aebischer, 2020, p. 175).

This explains why broadcast audiences, in response to a survey about watching an NT Live broadcast, 'reported higher levels of emotional engagement with the production than those who had experienced the play at the National Theatre' (NESTA, 2010, p. 5). Broadcasts facilitate a deep immersion in a performance and a profound investment in the emotional trajectory of the protagonists that does not depend on the ability to interact, respond or co-create, which requires more metatheatrical and ethical consciousness. For broadcast audiences, Erin Sullivan has argued, a sense of 'aliveness as an experiential and affective quality' is uncoupled from 'liveness' and 'embodied co-presence' (2018, p. 62). The feeling of community, as I suggested in my discussion of the watch party for Thomas Ostermeier's *Hamlet*, is generated by interactions with other audience members rather than with the performers.

Zoom, it turned out, is similar to theatre broadcasts insofar as it lends itself to replicating the technological proximity to a character, and the creation of an intimate and emotional bond with a performer that does not necessarily depend on direct address to the audience or participants' responsibility/response-ability. Instead, the audience's affective investment in a character may simply be the result of the 'camerawork' of the performer, as they frame themselves and change their position vis-à-vis their webcam to create the equivalent of mid-shots and close-ups (long shots are rare simply because they hinge on the depth of the performer's home 'studio'). With the frame of the Zoom windows roughly corresponding to the aspect ratio of most televisions and computer screens, and with Zoom's green-screen backgrounds making it possible for performers to inhabit static and sometimes (hardware permitting) moving environments, the Creation Theatre team found it comparatively easy to achieve a filmic look.

Some characters, in fact, remained entirely within the fictional *locus* of the performance and did not show any awareness of the audience. These characters were observable, as it were, from the outside, with the camerawork occasionally affording the technological and emotional proximity effects which traditional theatre broadcasts use to replace the mutual and co-creative bond between performers and audience in the shared space of the theatre.

The main beneficiaries of this technologically proximate treatment were Miranda and Ferdinand. Throughout the show, the lovers remained in a *locus* that was quite removed from any awareness of the audience even if the special technological privileges they were granted promoted the audience's investment in their plotline and emotional trajectory. Miranda was first introduced talking Prospero side-on, with the two performers sharing the same backdrop of a bank of surveillance television screens to create the illusion that they were in the same room (Figure 12). When Miranda did look into the webcam, she was clearly not addressing the audience but rather using one of Prospero's surveillance camera feeds to communicate with Caliban in his cave. That same mechanism then enabled her to observe and fall in love with Ferdinand, with whom she remained in a *locus* 'bubble' for the remainder of the show.

That bubble was strengthened by the use of three pre-recorded sequences, all of which were dedicated to the lovers and to their attempt to break out of their individual imprisonment and reach each other. In the first of these, the virtual backdrops made way for a real-life suburban back garden surrounded by high fences – the sort of back garden many of the spectators were confined to on sunny lockdown afternoons – into which Miranda stepped to search for Ferdinand. Having found him in a neighbouring garden, they communicated through a hole in the fence. When the lovers next met in Ferdinand's log-carrying scene, Miranda once more took the initiative to push against both social and Zoom conventions when, frustrated by the 'wall' separating their respective Zoom frames, she thrust her hand through the middle of the screen to propose to Ferdinand. To a little 'magical' ping on the soundtrack, an equivalent female hand appeared in his Zoom frame (Figure 13). With the barrier between them broken, the final pre-recorded psychedelic sequence showed the lovers video-edited to appear within a single Zoom frame, floating among fluffy white clouds while flower petals dropped down over them.

Reflecting on her approach to integrating pre-recorded material in the production, Seaton recalls how the storm scene in the Zoom show was initially going to be 'a beautiful film of a storm and I was like, no, it's died, the whole thing has died, it's gone' (interview, 6 July 2020). What might have been similarly 'dead' theatre in the Ferdinand-and-Miranda sequences

Figure 12 Miranda (Annabelle Terry) talking to her father (visible in a small box on the right in front of a matching green-screened background) within the *locus* of Prospero's cell. *The Tempest*, dir. Zoë Seaton for Creation Theatre and Big Telly, 2020.

Figure 13 Ferdinand (Ryan Duncan) and Miranda (Annabelle Terry) pushing through the boundaries of the Zoom platform. *The Tempest*, dir. Zoë Seaton for Creation Theatre and Big Telly, 2020.

was experienced as intensely live in part because of the audience's collective and contagious response of delight, and in part, too, because those sequences chimed so strongly with our deep longing to break out of the isolation of lockdown and touch one another.

In her conversation with John Wyver, Judith Buchanan (2020) comments on the sequence in which Miranda and Ferdinand break through the frame and touch each other and explains how that magical moment 'catches us. ... It plays to something that is a very deep craving. And it also ... emblematises something that is true of [the production] in relation to us' because this moment is 'inviting *us* to try and reach out, as well beyond those frames, to make a connection'. Heidi Liedke (2020), too, lingers on the 'emotional yearning' for community this scene provoked in her bearing witness to the power of pre-recorded material and a *locus* mode of performance to provoke strong affective responses that tie viewers to the emotional journeys travelled by central characters, without affording any response-ability on the part of the audience.

The fact that Miranda was so strongly associated with pre-recorded material and the *locus* she inhabited in her bubble with Ferdinand made her emergence from that *locus* in the final scene, when she finally spotted the audience on the other side of her webcam, the more moving:

> Oh, wonder!
> How many goodly creatures are there here!
> How beauteous mankind is! Oh, brave new world
> That has such people in't! (5.1.181–4)

These lines, addressed to the webcam, became the culmination of her quest for a world beyond the confines of her father's cell and the Zoom frame. Far from the cliché they have become, in the context of the first lockdown, Miranda's words acquired topical poignancy and emotional authenticity. They gave expression to the character's delight in having found a way of connecting with an entire gallery view full of people outside the desperate isolation of Prospero's island, who now joined her and the rest of the wedding guests in a wild and happy 1980s disco dance.

Unlike the lovers in their bubble, throughout the show the other characters made regular use of their webcams as a means of direct address to the audience, using the Zoom platform flexibly as a *locus* that also afforded casual *platea* moments that openly acknowledged the audience's presence. The performance opened with a 'press conference' in which audience members were invited to ask the royal party questions they had been sent via the chat function. The company thus used the platform in the mode of a webinar broadcast that structurally limited the audience's ability to respond even as it enabled them to feel seen. This set up the ground rules for audience interaction with the majority of the cast: the spectators were being seen, could occasionally be heard when asked directly to perform a task, but were confined to pre-scripted roles that conferred on them very circumscribed scope for their creative agency.

Once shipwrecked, the characters mainly interacted with one another rather than the audience. Still, they remained aware of the audience's presence, turning to their webcams with a knowing look for a quick moment of eye contact or addressing the viewers directly with an aside before continuing to talk to their scene partners. These they either addressed directly via their webcams or, more frequently, through an approximation of eyeline matches that used conventions borrowed from film to place them in a virtual shared space that was formally demarcated through a shared green-screened *mise-en-scène*. The platform, in other words, afforded a fluid approach to the audience-performer relationship that transposed the dynamics possible on the early modern platform stage to the digital stage, while keeping the audience's ability to respond (Lehmann's responsibility/response-ability) under the control of the cast.

2.1.3 'Canst thou remember / A time before we came unto this cell?': The 2020 Zoom *Tempest* as 'Flesh Memory'

What made the production stand out, however, were those interactions with the audience that burst through the digital 'fourth wall': the exuberant moments of co-creation Gillinson's (2020) review had highlighted when she wrote that 'it's the audience who are the most excited and exciting characters of all'. These brief but frequent moments of free-wheeling audience improvisation and performance were made possible by Sinéad Owens, the 'Zoom Wizard' behind the scenes/screens, selecting which individual spectators would be made visible to all viewers by using Zoom's 'spotlighting' feature. The spotlighting of performing spectators was one of the principal strategies through which the lockdown *Tempest* remembered and created a much more convincing archive of the previous year's analogue production, with its participatory theatricality, openness to serendipity and generation of a creative community, than the 2019 Facebook live stream could ever hope to be.

Some of that archiving was simply an effect of actors reprising their former roles and approach to characterisation and combining pieces of costume they or the company still owned with items from their own wardrobes that would give their characters a 'look' that was recognisably similar to Ryan Duncan-Laight's costume designs the previous year. This was even true for an actor like Giles Stoakley, whose previous part as the Ship Captain was cut and who moved into the role of Antonio. While Stoakley brought some of the Ship Captain's qualities as an organiser of audience responses to his role as press conference compère at the start of the show, his sartorial style and unconventional method of wearing his tie either on his head or upside-down when drowning further established visual connections between his former and current roles. Meanwhile, his approach to the role of Antonio, while not actually copying the performance of his predecessor, was informed by it insofar as it still had to fit in with the characterisation of his scene partner, Madeleine MacMahon in the role of Sebastian. While Stoakley insists that 'it would be unfair to call [the Zoom production] an archive of the live show' (email, 30 November 2020), his body nevertheless became what Rebecca Schneider would describe as 'a kind of archive' of these earlier performances, 'a *different approach to saving* that is not invested in identicality' (2001, p. 103, emphasis in original). The 2020 Zoom show, that is, while clearly a new production for a new medium, was also an embodied archive of the 2019 analogue production that saved key elements of it *differently*.

For the most part, however, it fell to Itxaso Moreno's Ariel in collaboration with the audience to catalyse the memory work of this production. It was Moreno, who had been such an elusive, disruptive figure in the 2019 production's Facebook live stream, who emerged once more as a disruptor in the Zoom production and as the principal source of analogue energy and embodied, ephemeral, elusive performativity. The circumstances of the pandemic lockdown, it was clear, had forced her Ariel to bend to Prospero's digital rule and have her face reproduced, seemingly infinitely and identically, in the bank of television screens lined up behind Prospero. However, even as this unruly spirit reluctantly allowed her image to be captured and reproduced, she did so with a profound investment in the analogue. As a result, she was the only character whose body was located not in the virtual environment of a two-dimensional Zoom background but was rooted deeply in the 'real' world of an understairs cupboard converted with the help of some fairy lights into Ariel's three-dimensional cave (Figure 14).

As Zoë Seaton recalled later, it was Moreno's profound technophobia that resulted in this adaptation: 'we just started trying to help her to build a space in her house which felt like Ariel's cave and for me that was more beautiful than any virtual background we could have had' (interview, 6 July 2020). Moreno's resistance to Zoom gave the whole production the intense sense of theatricality for which it garnered critical acclaim: having Ariel 'in a real space', Seaton acknowledges, 'gave us the key to that playful theatricality of how she was making a storm in a bowl in her room'. Liedke (2020) describes Moreno's Ariel as 'the bridge between fiction and reality, technology and materiality, "us" (the spectators) and "them" (the actors

Figure 14 Ariel (Itxaso Moreno) cooking up a storm in a bowl. *The Tempest*, dir. Zoë Seaton for Creation Theatre and Big Telly, 2020.

and actresses)'. Her rootedness in analogue theatrical magic allowed Moreno to reach out to spectators in their individual homes, engaging them in haptic, physical acts of co-creation. She involved us in creating the soundscape of the storm by rubbing our hands together and clapping, taunting the courtiers with the sort of food that was hard to obtain during lockdown (someone waved a packet of rice at their screen) or helping her be a whole flock of harpies screeching and flapping our wings at Antonio and Sebastian.

In orchestrating these moments of joyful audience improvisation and competition for the spotlight that made participants light up with an even bigger smile whenever they realised they were visible on-screen, Ariel produced the *'mutual implication of actors and spectators in the theatrical production of images'* which, as we saw, Lehmann posits as essential for the creation of an *'aesthetic of responsibility (or response-ability)'* that is truly theatrical (2006, pp. 185–6, emphasis in the original). Even when that responsibility/response-ability was (mis)used to torment an essentially innocent character such as Ferdinand, the experience was framed, within

Figure 15 Audience participation in Ferdinand's torture. With Rachael Nicholas' kind permission. *The Tempest*, dir. Zoë Seaton for Creation Theatre and Big Telly, 2020.

this utopian *Tempest*, as a comic piece of slapstick. Ferdinand being 'hit' in the groin by audience members flicking their fingers at him (Figure 15), rather than provoking unease and a sense of guilt at our complicity in Prospero's excessive use of his power, provided a moment of deliciously sadistic humour because of the transparent absurdity of the link between the cause and its disproportionate virtual effect.

While cramping Moreno into a cupboard literalised her character's confinement by Prospero and became an apt metaphor for the lockdown situation cast and audiences were painfully aware of, that very restriction also gave her irrepressibly physical performance additional power. She put the flesh on the bones of the Zoom production as an archival record and a live theatrical performance on a digital stage in its own right. Schneider speaks of how the performing body, rather than always already in the process of disappearing in the manner proposed by Phelan, can be 'resiliently eruptive, remaining through performance like so many ghosts at the door marked "disappeared"'. Indeed, 'performance becomes itself through messy and eruptive reappearance, challenging, via the performative trace, any neat antinomy between appearance and disappearance, or presence and absence' (Schneider 2001, p. 103). Moreno's Ariel purposefully opened up a portal between the analogue past and the digital present, bursting out of the Zoom frame as a force of live theatrical performativity to bring the audience's own bodies into (the) play, activating their muscle memory of participating in live theatre and being part of a creative community.

In the end, much of the archiving work through which the 2020 Zoom production remembered its precursor and brought it back into the company's repertoire was arguably carried out by the audience themselves. In her consideration of what cognitive science has taught us about mirror neurons, Amy Cook suggests that recognising how the 'real actions' of the performers 'prompt a co-firing' of mirror neurons 'in the spectator's brain' enables us to appreciate the extent to which the theatrical experience depends on the 'coherence of the group created by imitation': 'Acting in synchrony with others, based on the interplay of social conventions and spontaneous feelings, unites spectator with spectator as it also co-fires mirror neurons' (2009, p. 113). For Cook, this insight 'shifts focus from the imitation of an action by an actor to the imitation of a performed action by the spectators watching the performance' (2009, p. 114). In this understanding of how theatre works as 'flesh memory' (Cook, 2009, p. 108; Schneider, 2001, p. 105), the power of memorialising a prior performance is given not just to the actors but also to the audience. The spectators' embodied responses, whether in the shape of mirror neurons triggered by watching the actors perform or actual physical movement in synchrony with other audience members, are crucial.

In the Zoom *Tempest* performances, the visible participation of other spectators in the action was a vital component of how the production produced an embodied memory of the experience of live participatory theatre as a communal creative act. This was the opposite of the disconnection from fellow audience members I felt when watching Teller and Posner's *Macbeth* at the Folger Shakespeare Library with a North American 'home' audience or Thomas Ostermeier's *Hamlet* with an Anglophone watch party. Where those broadcasts had produced feelings of isolation and even alienation, watching *The Tempest*, by contrast, produced an experience of hyperconnection with fellow audience members joining in from their separate homes. In almost magical synchrony we came together to shake our screens, flap our arms and screech or dance at Miranda's wedding.

Despite the geographical separation of spectators watching the show from twenty-seven countries (Aebischer and Nicholas, 2020a, p. 33), in this virtual *platea* spectators and actors mingled and interacted, recognised acquaintances joining in from faraway places and waved at each other as if across a busy auditorium. In doing so, the *Tempest* audience performed in the synchronous manner which Robert Shaughnessy has observed in audiences and performers in Shakespeare's Globe Theatre, a performance environment that similarly favours the *platea*. The 'entrainment' Shaughnessy describes in Globe audiences connects actors and spectators through an experience of synchrony which results in audiences experiencing 'higher levels of engagement with Shakespeare' (2020, p. 28).

Similarly, more than three-quarters of the viewers we surveyed for *Digital Theatre Transformation* found that interaction and being able to see other audience members was important to them, with 86.3 per cent reporting that watching the show had made them feel part of a community (Aebischer and Nicholas, 2020b). The 'entrainment' Shaughnessy observes at Shakespeare's Globe is, arguably, a constitutive factor in what W. B. Worthen describes as 'Globe performativity': 'a participatory *experience* of the past in a mode of performance designed to be pervasive, incorporating the audience in a virtual society, a landscape, an engulfing atmosphere' (Worthen, 2003, p. 83, emphasis in original). What this *Tempest* modelled might therefore be termed 'Zoom performativity': a participatory experience of a past mode of theatrical performance in a new medium designed to pervasively incorporate the audience and their home environment in a virtual society, a shared virtual landscape, an engulfing atmosphere of life-affirming community building. *The Tempest* thus enabled performers and audience to remember a time before they came into the cell of their individual Zoom frames through their embodied participation in playing together.

The show's curtain call reinforced that visceral bonding between cast and audience and between audience members, as one performer after another dismantled their green screen set-up and revealed the insides of their homes. That revelation of themselves as actors who had all abjured their magic and were now meeting the audience as equals exposed their and the audience's mutual vulnerability, as they could see and be seen as their private selves in their domestic environments. With dance music blaring on the soundtrack, cast and audience came together in gallery view, still dancing, waving and clapping, as a community of individuals in lockdown celebrating through their synchronous applause the successful conclusion of a live theatrical performance. The curtain call provoked complicated feelings of yearning for community, wallowing in the warmth of momentary togetherness and a reluctance to leave the call and be plunged back into the lonesomeness of lockdown, which appeared almost the greater for having been reminded of what it felt like to be part of something, to see and be seen.

2.2 Hecate Rules: *Big Telly's* Macbeth

2.2.1 'Something Wicked This Way Comes': Zoom Performativity in the Service of Dystopia

Zoë Seaton returned to Shakespeare under the banner of Big Telly (Northern Ireland) in the autumn of 2020 to produce *Macbeth* for the Belfast International Arts Festival (14–17 October). That festival appearance was followed by a ten-day virtual 'tour' to Oxford, where they were hosted by the Creation Theatre box office and platform until the run's final performance at midnight on Halloween (31 October).[17] By this point, Seaton's core team of stage manager (Sinéad Owens), producer (Crissy O'Donovan, seconded by Creation Theatre) and Giles Stoakley (production manager) had accrued more than half a year of experience working together with the Zoom platform. They had collaborated not just on *The Tempest* but also on *Alice: A Virtual Theme Park*, a co-production with Creation Theatre in August 2020 for which the companies joined forces with digital interactive storytelling experts Charisma AI, which pushed their work ever further into an intermedial domain.

While *Alice*'s reviews were strong, the show's timing was unfortunate. *Alice* coincided with low Covid-19 case numbers in the United Kingdom,

---

[17] The show was revived in November 2020, when it 'travelled' to The Red Curtain Good The@ter Festival & Awards in Kolkata, India.

the easing of lockdown restrictions and the chancellor's 'Eat Out to Help Out' scheme, which encouraged families to spend their leisure time either outdoors or having a half-price meal in a pub or restaurant. The unambiguous 'Stay At Home – Protect the NHS – Save Lives' public health message on the prime minister's lectern during daily press briefings from Downing Street had now been replaced by 'Stay Alert – Control the Virus – Save Lives' – a slogan which provoked much mockery for its vagueness (Clarke, 2020). The transition from a springtime of discontent to glorious summer resulted in slumping ticket sales for *Alice*, testing the companies' confidence in the commercial viability of digital theatre.

By the autumn, however, the weather had turned again, the nights were drawing in, the 'Eat Out to Help Out' scheme and re-opening of schools had led to a rise in Covid-19 infections (Fetzer, 2020, p. 6; Sample and Davis, 2020), and a second lockdown was predictably imminent. The leader of the opposition was calling on the UK's prime minister to impose a 'circuit-breaker' lockdown during the October half-term school break in England to stop the virus spreading. For the third time since March 2020, a trip to visit my parents was cancelled because of safety concerns, and my family's conversations turned to the question of pumpkin carving and how best to make sure that some of the rituals of Halloween at the end of the 'staycation' half-term break could take place in a 'Covid-secure' way.

Seaton's *Macbeth* emerged within this context as the dystopian counterpart to the utopian spirit of *The Tempest*, whose model of 'Zoom performativity' had expressed a joyful belief in the ability of theatre to transport audiences and performers into a virtual community, and thereby to uplift and inspire optimism about our ability to overcome Covid-19 through the sheer power of our collective creativity. The marketing for *Macbeth*, by way of contrast, made the most of the seasonal obsession with witchcraft and suspicion of strangers at the door. With an age rating of 14+ and a trailer whose black-and-white footage, heavy breathing and extreme close-ups of faces evoked the cult low-budget horror film *The Blair Witch Project*, the production clearly targeted teen and adult audiences who were looking for a 'Covid-secure' alternative way of marking Halloween.

All the learning the company had done on the Zoom platform was now deployed to '[subvert] what audiences [had] come to expect from virtual theatre' (Broadribb, 2021a). Seaton herself is very clear on this: 'We arrived at *Macbeth* as a production team ready to tackle this play in a way that we wouldn't have been six months earlier – technically, emotionally or conceptually. I wouldn't have put *Macbeth* on in March, because people needed joy not darkness' (cited in Allred and Broadribb, 2022, forthcoming). Accordingly, the show drew on its experienced Zoom audience's expertise and their expectation of joyful participatory Zoom performativity to build discomfort and shock into the experience of the show and wrong-foot their viewers. In line with Seaton's enthusiasm for how Zoom enables creatives to tell stories that are 'about now' (cited in Allred and Broadribb, 2022, forthcoming), her *Macbeth* unnervingly tapped into the growing awareness of how the public health measures to combat the pandemic had led to 'alarming increases in domestic violence and mental health problems' both in the United Kingdom and worldwide (Lambert et al., 2020, p. e313). The production was fuelled by the public mood of suspicion of public health messaging, distrust of politicians' handling of the pandemic, despondence at the signs of a second Covid-19 wave and the sense of threat stemming from the intrusion of potentially contagious trick-or-treating strangers into our homes.

2.2.2 'Fair is foul and foul is fair': *Macbeth* as a Covid-19 Carnival

Key to the production's topical dystopianism was its investment in the carnivalesque and inversion of norms that is intrinsic to the Halloween season. What Mikhail Bakhtin in his discussion of carnival calls 'grotesque realism' foregrounds the body's penetrability and leakiness and gives particular weight to 'those parts of the body that are open to the outside world, that is, the parts through which the world enters the body or emerges from it, or through which the body itself goes out to meet the world' (Bakhtin, 1984, pp. 19, 26). The grotesque body of carnival, in other words, is a body that is intrinsically contagious and itself open to contamination.

Bakhtin sees this carnivalesque as profoundly celebratory and triggering laughter because of the cyclical nature of life and death, and the ways in which the grotesque body, even as it is marked by death, is 'also regenerating ... always conceiving' (Bakhtin, 1984, p. 21). Reading

Bakhtin, Renate Lachmann concludes that the 'principle of laughter' that underpins his conception of the carnival is informed by the paradigms of 'instability, openness and infiniteness, the metamorphotic, ambivalence, the eccentric, materiality and corporeality, [and] the exchange of value positions (up/down, master/slave)' (Lachmann, 1988–1989, p. 136). Bakhtin's carnival, through that exchange of value positions and its levelling spirit, is also a mode of anti-institutional, parodic political critique that involves 'the intercrossing of official discourses ... with the unofficial discourse of folk culture', such as the ghost and witchcraft lore of Halloween (Lachmann, 1988–1989, p. 142). Crucially, too, carnival is participatory and communal: it hinges on the individual's 'entrance into the space of the transindividual carnival community' (Lachmann, 1988–1989, p. 142).

Such a participatory entrance into a shared carnivalesque space was facilitated at the start of *Macbeth* by a 'Daily Briefing' held in a virtual approximation of Downing Street's improvised press room, with three lecterns for the 'Prime Minister', the 'Chief Scientific Adviser' and the 'Minister for the Economy' (Figure 16). The briefing involved the Prime Minister spouting platitudes about 'living in unprecedented times' and needing to 'be vigilant' (a clear dig at the vagueness of Prime Minister Boris Johnson's 'be alert' message). Meanwhile, the Minister for the Economy requested that his audience should 'refrain from any practices which might involve imagination, innovation and creativity during these difficult times' and offered a reminder that 'theatres must remain closed for the foreseeable future'.

The political skit also included the Chief Scientific Adviser carrying out a screening process of audience members, who were asked to hold up handwritten 'location cards' on which they had written the name of the place from where they were joining in the show. The featured spectators were then 'screened' for signs of exposure to witchcraft. When some spectators tested positive, a second screening then declared the initial test result to have been a 'false positive', playing on the emerging distrust of 'lateral flow' Covid-19 tests that needed to be verified by laboratory PCR tests. This then enabled the Chief Scientific Adviser to highlight the carnivalesque topsy-turvydom of pandemic terminology with a reminder that the 'positive result ... is, of course, a negative thing'.

Figure 16 The Chief Scientific Adviser (Lucia McAnespie), the Prime Minister (Aonghus Óg McAnally) and the Minister of the Economy (Dharmesh Patel) at the Daily Briefing. *Macbeth*, dir. Zoë Seaton for Big Telly, 2020.

The audience was thus welcomed into a creative community of people who courted danger by virtue of indulging in communal acts of theatrical creativity. The opening gambit raised expectations of the type of participatory Zoom performativity to which spectators had grown accustomed over the preceding months. The opening up of a *platea* space of direct interaction seemed to invite viewers to join in a 'transindividual carnival community' that would offer satirical relief from the deadly serious quotidian ritual of Downing Street press briefings.

Yet there was also something profoundly unnerving already in this first carnivalesque take on the pandemic: the manner in which the company had 'hacked' Zoom by means of a live video-mixing software to bring the three performers into a shared virtual space was disconcerting in its clunkiness. The torsos of the performers were truncated above the lecterns in slightly different sizes, giving them a legless marionette-like feel. The scene triggered the 'eerie sensation' of the 'uncanny valley' first identified by

Masahiro Mori ([1970] 2012, p. 199), whereby viewers suffer visceral 'discomfort or even revulsion' at the sight of a humanoid object that fails to entirely conform to human physiology (Bloom, 2018, p. 189).

That unsettling sensation carried on into the next scene when, the briefing concluded, shaky 'first-person' handheld camera footage, in a pre-recorded sequence, travelled through the backstage areas of an empty theatre (Brighton's Theatre Royal). Arrived in the dressing room, the three politicians were unmasked as the witches, in their natural habitat of a theatre where their bodies became congruent again. Here, the 'uncanny valley' effect made way for a different sort of cognitive disjunction. Because the witches used the Zoom camera as a mirror to touch up their make-up and adjust their costume for their first meeting with Macbeth and Banquo, the set-up logically suggested that when we were meeting the witches' eyes in the screen that was also a mirror, we were looking at (a version of) ourselves. Not only were the country's leaders revealed as witches, but *we*, the audience, were ourselves transformed into those witches, binding us into a visual identity with the play's instruments of disorder.

When, in the witches' confrontation with Macbeth and Banquo (Figure 17), Dharmesh Patel, who played one of the witches, also doubled as Banquo in conversation with himself, the grotesque porousness of bodies that could assume multiple, conflicting identities and split into *Doppelgänger* figures within a single scene, assumed a new peak. Technically, of course, the doubling of actors was simply a question of economics, of how many performers the company could afford to pay. However, conceptually and affectively, too, the doubling, tripling and even quadrupling of roles played by the trio of Patel, Lucia McAnespie and Aonghus Óg McAnally, who between them performed all the characters save for Macbeth (Dennis Herdman) and Lady Macbeth (Nicky Harley), fed into the production's sinister deployment of the carnivalesque. Lachmann explains how carnivalesque doublings and *Doppelgänger* figures signal an 'ambivalence in the person' in which 'the body ... becomes the stage for eccentricity. It is the body that transgresses its own boundaries, that plays up its own exaggeration: the grotesque body' (Lachmann, 1988–1989, p. 146). Because many of the scenes involving the witches, in their different incarnations, were 'shared' with the audience from the screen of 'Hecate' (stage manager

Figure 17 The three witches (Aonghus Óg McAnally, Dharmesh Patel and Lucia McAnespie). *Macbeth*, dir. Zoë Seaton for Big Telly, 2020.

Sinéad Owens), the ability of these 'weird sisters' to morph into different characters who were often green-screened into their environments in a way that triggered the 'uncanny valley' effect was associated with the super-natural threat hanging over the play.

Obscene *Macbeth*

The creepiness of the uncanny valley effect and the ambivalence of recycled bodies intensified when viewers themselves were green-screened into the virtual environments in later participatory moments in a way that made the viewers' own bodies grotesque. The technological hacking of the Zoom platform, at those moments, worked as a powerful tool of estrangement from an interface most audience members were now using daily for work and leisure, introducing a sense of defamiliarising, sinister magic into the production. Most notably, this happened when viewers were integrated as dinner guests in Macbeth's coronation feast where Banquo's ghost appeared, or when they were featured as spectators in the private box at the theatre in which Macbeth encountered the apparition of the line of kings, which again included members of the audience each seated on their own outsized virtual chair. Herdman comments: 'There's a certain roughness to the live element. ... You see sort of disembodied heads at a banquet, and that's a bit weird – but good, and intriguing.' The world Herdman describes as 'very sort of "cut and paste"' provoked an underlying sense of unease at the bizarreness of the bodies of audience members on display, whose dimensions were out of kilter with the chairs they were virtually sitting on (Herdman in Allred and Broadribb, 2022, forthcoming).

As an experienced Zoom spectator who had joyfully participated in previous Creation Theatre and Big Telly shows, when I was spotlighted as a dinner guest at the Macbeths' feast, my excitement at being selected quickly gave way to profound awkwardness and a peculiar sensation of disembodiment. I had trouble mentally mapping my own body onto the diminutive on-screen version and was viscerally disgusted by the weirdness of my size in relation to the height of the table and the 'chair' I was sitting on. I simply did not know what to do with myself or how best to contribute to this scene. Being 'included' and watching myself as a badly performing actor made me acutely aware of the identity theft the production was performing by inserting me in it in this manner against my will. (Of course, it was with my consent: I still had the choice of switching my camera off – but could I really do that *while* I was also sitting at the virtual banquet? So embarrassing!) Being snatched out of the environment of my room and thrust into a different space transformed the benign voyeurism that is inherent in Zoom performativity, in which audiences all share their respective home environments with one another and allow others glimpses of a private life that is joyfully shared, into a malign body-snatching intrusion into my home space.

This, therefore, was not the *platea* experience of co-creative and mutually empowering theatrical communality that I had enjoyed in *The Tempest*, where I'd happily danced with a toy rabbit at the wedding disco. Instead, spotlighting in the central scenes of *Macbeth* worked in the manner of the obscene/ob-scene in the early modern theatre: the mode of spectatorship that neither observes performers contained in the *locus* nor allows spectators to enter into the mutual exchanges possible on the *platea* but that is triggered by glimpses of the offstage transgressive acts associated with the so-called discovery space at the back of the stage. This mode of spectatorship 'demands of its viewers a projection of their sight and/or imagination into the recesses of the playhouse to bring forth the "truths" that underpin the plays'; it involves an act of intrusion that activates the spectators' obscene imagination as they complement what they can see with what they can only infer (Aebischer, 2020, p. 19).

Spotlighting in *Macbeth* made the obscene operate, as it were, in reverse: instead of affording glimpses into the offstage spaces of the spectators' homes and making the other viewers project their imaginations into those homes to unearth what hidden 'truths' they might contain, the obscenity here lay in the forceful ripping of the spectator out of the safety of their homes and their virtual insertion into the world of the play. Each one of us became an intruder in the banquet who also acted as a 'portal' into a 'real' world beyond the fictional world of the play. It turned viewers into changelings within the Zoom space: alien creatures who disrupted that space, and whose faces and emotions were opened up to the intrusive, obscene imaginings of our fellow spectators. We never looked more apart and isolated than when we were sharing a virtual space. Rather than joyful community, the scene illustrated the effect of oxymoronic 'social distance': the separation of individuals in which social activity is only possible while staying rigorously distant from one another.

I suspect I was not alone in being troubled by this experience. Heidi Liedke and Monika Pietrzak-Franger thought that the invitations to participate in the production were 'associated with the pressure of "acting right" and not making an embarrassment of oneself' (2021, p. 138). What I experienced was a more acute feeling of being instrumentalised by the production to contribute to the scene's overall thematic engagement with the supernatural and the presence or absence, visibility and invisibility of the spectral figure of Banquo, who was similarly green-screened into the scene. The other spotlighted spectators in the performances I participated in also looked uneasy as they tentatively raised glasses or mugs that tended to disappear into the virtual background or tried on facial expressions appropriate to the moment. Notably, in one performance I saw, the repeated glitching of the green screen for a member of the audience with a dark skin tone, the contours of whose face were melting into the background, added to the unease provoked by the scene and the racial bias built into the Zoom technology (Costley 2020). If I felt disconcerted by my glitching hair, how did my fellow spectator feel about the dissolution of the contours of their face?

In his theorisation of the digital glitch, Michael Betancourt defines 'the aura of the digital' as based on 'the illusion of a self-productive domain, infinite, capable of creating value without expenditure, unlike the reality of limited resources, time, expense, etc. that otherwise govern all forms of value and production' (2017, p. 15). Digital stoppages and glitches have the capacity to rupture this aura and expose the medium's constructedness and the labour that is habitually obscured by the aura of the digital. Rather than being mere epiphenomena that could be disregarded as unfortunate side effects of the medium, the glitches in *Macbeth* ruptured the experience of the performance. They thus drew attention to the medium of Zoom not so much as the utopian means of overcoming distance and transforming our homes into cultural spheres from where we could enjoy theatre together but rather as a potentially harmful means of alienating us from our own bodies and creating a rigorously compartmentalised understanding of 'society' as 'socially distanced'.

These glitches were not deliberately pre-programmed by the production, but they were embraced by it to expose the materiality of the digital artwork, the *theatricality* of its 'rough magic'. If read as a simple 'technical failure', the digital glitch 'is noise that decomposes the apparent "perfection" of the commercial work'. If, instead, the glitch is transformed 'into a signifier for materiality', then it can be reframed in terms of illusion (Betancourt, 2017, p. 60). It can, that is, be read as the digital counterpart to the kind of theatrical magic which was, in this production, associated with the witches who inhabited the obscene, part-visible, part-hidden offstage spaces in the wings of the empty Theatre Royal from where they orchestrated the burlesque prophecy of Macbeth's invulnerability and the line of Kings. The glitches that characterised the audience's technological insertion into the virtual banquet, in other words, were discomforting in their connection with the theatrical obscene and their triggering of uncanny valley effects. They were also, crucially, deconstructive of the medium of Zoom as a theatrical platform in revealing its materiality and the production's rootedness in theatrical labour that demanded to be *noticed* and *paid for*. A platform whose commercial value lies in a slick social experience of togetherness, and whose stock price had soared by 268 per cent between 23 March (the day of the lockdown announcement) and 12 October 2020,[18] as all the world had seemingly become a Zoom stage, was mined for its potential to be hacked into. Zoom's weaknesses were exposed in the interests of foregrounding human agency, disempowerment, and the material(ist) underpinnings of virtual togetherness.

The obscene dynamic that thus infected the *platea* moments of the production also contaminated its representation of characters contained in the *locus*, notably Lady Macbeth and Lady Macduff (Lucia McAnespie). The male characters in the play were able to move fluently between indoor and outdoor spaces and between *locus* and *platea* modes of engagement with one another and with the spectators. Herdman's Macbeth even gaily waved back at waving spotlighted spectators from his coronation carriage to the Queen tune 'We Are the Champions'. But this freedom was not one enjoyed by the women in the play, whose minds and bodies were vulnerable and who were confined to homes that were portrayed as dangerous places that were also startlingly real and familiar, due to their being the home spaces of the performers (no male performer's home was used as a set).

Lady Macbeth was presented from the start as the fictional equivalent of the locked-down audience. During the Daily Briefing, a brief shot of Nicky Harley lying on a bed and watching the briefing on her laptop reflected the audience's own experience of watching the same broadcast from their respective homes before audiences could identify her as Lady Macbeth. In striking contrast with the uncanny virtual environments of the Daily Briefing and the witches' subsequent encounter with Macbeth, throughout the first half of the play Lady Macbeth was shown in the domestic setting of an attic bedroom in Harley's home. That room was connected to the front door of the house through several flights of stairs she rushed down to pick up Macbeth's letter. Switching between the video feeds of a handheld camera to track that movement and several cameras dotted around her

---

[18] See www.statista.com/statistics/1106104/stock-price-zoom/, figures checked 24 August 2021.

bedroom afforded separate viewpoints onto her and offered a viewing experience akin to that of a multi-camera theatre broadcast that afforded technological proximity and emotional access even as it locked the character into the production's *locus*.

Whereas a theatre broadcast would work to construct a spatially coherent environment for the viewer, however, Seaton's production, while tantalising its audience with the promise of spatial coherence, virtual co-presence and eyeline matches, ultimately frustrated that desire. Seaton's own comments on her approach to the spatial naturalism of screen media are revealing:

> There are several times in this where we could have achieved naturalism, but is that worth fighting for? ... That point where you go, 'Are we just making crap TV?' Let's not do that! Let's try and expose the process more. For act 2 scene 3, we needed everyone in the Macbeths' hallway – we had many different attempts at how to make that work. We had so many photos of people's homes we 'auditioned', so many front doors and driveways. And then we said, 'Well, what we actually need from that is a sense of place, but we don't need to be ... killed by our own rules, we can break these rules, and I like breaking rules.
>
> (Seaton in Allred and Broadribb, 2022, forthcoming)

Seaton's willingness to break with televisual conventions and embrace spatial incoherence translated into an incongruous hallway in which the same door led to different exteriors and people on the stairs and landings were in impossible spatial relationships to one another. In Lady Macbeth's bedroom, too, the arrival of Macbeth, who was virtually inserted into a corner of the room that did not fit with either its dimensions or the time of day (it was daytime when he was there, night-time when she was in the shot), upset spatial and temporal logic, giving the room an 'unnervingly surreal aesthetic' (Broadribb, 2021b). That spatio-temporal logic came under further attack in Lady Macbeth's descent into madness, when the simple Zoom trick of draping a blanket around her neck made it possible for snatches of the banquet hall to be green-screened into the bedroom environment, so that the character was simultaneously inhabiting two spatio-temporal zones and dragging the past into the present (Figure 18). These scenes, as a consequence, triggered obscene modes of spectatorship marked by the desire to look into and understand Harley's home, how the Macbeths were able to coexist in it, and to peer into the dark corners of her bedroom.

Some of the ever more extreme close-ups on her face in the central scenes leading up to and following on from Duncan's murder furthermore offered an obscene access to the dark corners of Lady Macbeth's mind. As she moved ever closer to both the crime and the Zoom camera and her mind began to fracture, Harley's Lady Macbeth moved so close to her webcam that her face was fragmented into its outsized component parts. With her snot and tears mingling in the manner of Bakhtin's 'open', leaky, grotesque carnivalesque body, we saw into the inside of her mouth and nostrils and

Figure 18 Lady Macbeth (Nicky Harley) in her bedroom, draped in the virtual environment of the banquet hall. *Macbeth*, dir. Zoë Seaton for Big Telly, 2020.

could observe the smudging of her make-up by the tears in the single scrunched-up eye that filled the screen.

That the character was unaware of the viewer's all-too-intimate access to her body augmented the obscene intimacy of those scenes: the camera's eye was probing the soft, moist fleshiness of her orifices, exposing Lady Macbeth's insides to public view in her most private moments in a manner that was both compelling and repulsive. When, her mind cracked open, Lady Macbeth strode into the black-and-white Irish Sea in her bright red ball gown, her insertion in a big, open landscape and the respectful distance of the camera in this pre-recorded sequence translated into a hauntingly beautiful sense of liberation from the oppressiveness of intruding gazes and her locked-down domestic prison (Figure 19).

At first, Lady Macduff's home appeared to offer some respite from the incoherence of Lady Macbeth's house and mind. With Lady Macduff feeding a baby on her sofa while watching her husband appear in the television news bulletin, the naturalistic television grammar presented

Figure 19 Lady Macbeth (Nicky Harley). *Macbeth*, dir. Zoë Seaton for Big Telly, 2020. Production photograph © Sinéad Owens.

a picture of a spatially coherent, harmonious household. The fact that this scene of happy domesticity was attributed to 'Hecate' provided an early indication that the sinister forces at work, however, and our awareness that we were afforded a tour of the performer's own home that included a brief appearance by her little daughter, who sweetly asked 'where's Daddy?', added to the sense of unease.[19]

As the scene progressed, the camerawork and soundtrack increasingly borrowed the tropes of horror film, contaminating this *locus*, too, with the qualities of the obscene: handheld camera footage peering into the home from outside the kitchen window and moving towards the mother and baby signalled the presence of an intruder. The more Lady Macduff, to the sound of a lullaby, moved around her house to close the doors of children's bedrooms, shut the curtains and lower her blinds, the more inevitable her murder became. A child's scream made her rush up the stairs, where she froze wide-eyed before tumbling down to the landing. The camera obscenely lingered on her broken body, the thick blood grotesquely gurgling out of her stomach wound, and on the open eyes that sightlessly peered back at the sofa that had signified safety and contentment. What had begun as a fun indulgence of the carnivalesque spirit of Halloween was, through 'Hecate's' mediation, transformed into the horror of death intruding into locked-down homes to wipe out an entire family.

At the end of the performance, the jaunty music of burlesque theatre and the actors' curtain call with their own 'location cards' showing that they, too, were geographically separate worked to rekindle the more joyful spirit of Lachmann's 'transindividual carnival community'. In the centre of the show, however, Seaton's embrace of the rough edges of vision mixing, her deliberate breaking of the rules of naturalism and the resulting obscene and uncanny effects allowed her production to tap into something much more troubling in its exploration of Zoom as the theatrical medium of choice for the time of pandemic. Her Halloween *Macbeth* quite brilliantly made the everyday interface of Zoom

---

[19] McAnespie herself recorded her disquiet when she admitted that 'there's just no way that we could do [that scene with her daughter] live every night, my nerves just couldn't take it!' (McAnespie in Allred and Broadribb, 2022a, forthcoming).

a dangerous space, in which the medium's ability to penetrate into the home spaces of participants was revealed to be potentially malign.

Where *The Tempest* had revolved around the magical moment of Miranda and Ferdinand reaching through the boundaries of their respective Zoom frames to touch, the defining moments of *Macbeth* were those where characters could not reach one another, audiences were included as 'changelings', spaces were disorienting and homes were unsafe. More than anything else, the theatrical framing of the production, its association of Zoom wizardry with the backstage labour of theatre workers, and the circular structure that took us from spotlighted audience members proffering their location cards to the cast doing the same at the end of the show, created a community of equals brought together through shared precarity. Each participant, in their separate location, was faced with their individual vulnerability to violence, illness, isolation, cultural deprivation, invisibility of their labour, loss of their livelihood and potential for mental disintegration.

The curtain call reunited a community of people who had performed the very acts of creativity, innovation and imagination which the show's Minister of the Economy had pinpointed as posing a risk of contagion and which the UK's lord chancellor had structurally sidelined in the Cultural Recovery Fund's lack of provision for freelancers. Its aesthetic of response-ability/responsibility recast audiences as fellow actors in what Judith Butler, in her reflections on the forms of protest available to people who have been deemed 'ungrievable' and whose lives therefore receive no protection through inclusion in policies, describes as 'a form of theatrical politics'. Asserting their existence through theatrical acts of protest that assert power while acknowledging 'the limits imposed on power at the same time' enables those whose survival is not secured by any policy to engage in performative acts of defiance. Even if 'the slogan is simply "we exist"', that assertion serves to 'break through the denial that these are lives, that they deserve recognition, support, and legal status, and that they can be lost' (Butler, 2021, pp. 183, 184).

Macbeth, similarly, by foregrounding theatrical labour and asserting the existence of a theatrical community that shared the screen at the end of the show, performed an act of political defiance that acknowledged the closure of the theatres while asserting the power and presence of performers and their audiences. In the dystopian setting of an empty theatre, Seaton's *Macbeth* offered a form of theatrical protest that, through the simple act of performing on a digital stage, asserted the continued existence of performers and sought to break through the denial that acting is a livelihood that deserves fiscal recognition and support, and that these jobs can be lost.

At least we'll die with harness on our back. (*Macbeth*, 5.5.52)

Conclusion: When Will This Fearful Slumber Have an End?

As I wrap up this journal of my pandemic year, we are halfway through the second year of Covid. The precariousness of the theatre industry has only intensified since October 2020: more theatres have shut and companies folded. Theatre broadcasts are no longer available as free online streams, and when there is a broadcast, it is likely to be a ticketed live stream of a new production involving a small cast of performers in a theatre without an audience in the room. Some companies are moving outdoors and tentatively scheduling new live shows, but the cultural news cycle is filled with accounts of shows having to be cancelled because a member of the cast has tested positive for Covid-19.

Since the second lockdown of November 2020, my viewing schedule has calmed down: it is now equivalent to how often I used to watch theatre before the pandemic. Yet I have not returned to a theatre building, and my group of watch party friends has expanded to include people in Switzerland, Germany, Northern Ireland, Canada and the United States, expert at negotiating time zones to watch a show together and chat about it afterwards. What would have been unthinkable at the start of 2020 has become almost – but not entirely – normal, with new rituals and habits, including the obligatory wave at the camera at the end of a show. But I miss the pre-theatre dinners, the physical discomfort mixed with excitement as we find our way to our seats, the smell of a packed auditorium, the scent of spotlights or beeswax candles, the soreness of my applauding hands, trying to catch the eye of the performer I am applauding, the jostle as we head out to get a drink. I miss theatre less than I miss paratheatre. The buildings may have been shut, but thanks to the creativity of companies nimble and imaginative enough to keep the digital lights on, *performance* never stopped in the time of pandemic.

When restrictions on outdoor performances eased in July 2021, Big Telly's Zoë Seaton seized the opportunity to reconnect with analogue audiences in Northern Ireland through immersive games–inspired outdoor productions without abandoning the company's digital discoveries. Big Telly is now exploring hybrid modes of performance that give both in-person and digital audiences 'complementary LIVE experiences of equal value' and enable both types of audiences the ability to influence the performance. 'This new hybrid way of working', O'Donovan explains, 'is born out of the digital revolution we embarked on during the pandemic and the shared community we gathered because of it' (email, 29 June 2021).

In Oxford meanwhile, Creation Theatre's Lucy Askew is leading her company, which before the pandemic was specialising in site-specific promenade performances in 'found' locations, in the direction of ever more innovative digital partnerships and explorations, with ever more diverse performers in leading roles. Following the award of Innovate UK funding, the company has been collaborating with two tech companies, Flipside and Charisma AI, to develop their own digital theatre platform and take the 'hacking' of Zoom one step further towards independence from that commercial template and its market dominance.

Zoom, in the course of the pandemic and following reports of 'Zoom bombing' of meetings (unauthorised participants appearing on screens, inappropriate content being shared) and safeguarding concerns, tightened its security settings and, in doing so, restricted the use of some of the features which had made the platform such a convenient stage at first. Notably, the ability of a host to unmute all participants and thus enable a whole audience to applaud or make other noises together, was disabled soon after the run of *The Tempest*, making that type of participatory theatre more challenging to produce on Zoom. Creation Theatre's aim for its new platform is to free itself from such constraints and build a stage that is safe, intuitive and participatory, and more environmentally sustainable than analogue theatre, too. Askew's ultimate goal is to establish a hybrid mode of working for Creation Theatre that will enable the company to weather future shocks, whether pandemic or climate related.

That the company should be attempting to build its own digital stage is a sign of the extent to which digital theatre has evolved in the course of the pandemic year, and also of an increasing awareness of how the headlong embrace of a range of social media – not just Zoom but also other platforms such as Twitter (the main watch party platform), WhatsApp (*The Merry Wives of WhatsApp* was a satire that hit a genuine lockdown nerve), Tiktok, YouTube, Facebook, and so on – risked compromising the safety and data of users. Rather than neutral tools for communication, these platforms exploit our thirst for participatory cultural activities to harvest information about our interests and preferences and target their advertising, while also contributing to the polarisation of society and the creation of 'echo chambers' in which users are ever more consistently exposed only to information that accords with their own previously stated opinions. Cultural participation via social media platforms controlled by data-mining algorithms can thus lead to an exacerbation of political divisions and promote specific public health messages and potential misinformation. It is not for nothing that the pandemic has been accompanied by what the United Nations has termed an 'infodemic', that is, a pandemic spread of misinformation or disinformation that may be as dangerous as the Covid-19 virus itself (United Nations, 2020).

Many viewers of digital Shakespeare shows, while aware of the dangers inherent in the use of these platforms, have nevertheless embraced those substitute modes of social and cultural participation. Many of us have relied on our common sense to avoid 'herd thinking' while knowing full well that the systems we use are designed to counter individualism and to foster addictive behaviour. My own experience and markedly increased use of Twitter for the purposes of joining watch parties, embrace of Zoom for work and leisure and use of WhatsApp for private group chats speaks to the increasingly seductive power of social media at a time of social isolation and their ability to use cultural activity as a means of creating and consolidating social siloes. I have greatly enjoyed the formation of groups of like-minded individuals who enjoy watching Shakespeare together and also 'happen to' share the same views regarding public health messaging, racial equality, higher education policy, the climate emergency and politics (all of which sharply divide opinion in the wider world) – but how unmediated and natural are these groups?

I have also recoiled from groups whose opinions did not align directly with mine. Not sharing the enjoyment of the stage magic and kilts for Teller and Posner's *Macbeth*, and therefore feeling ill at ease in the Folger's Shakespeare Theater's watch party and leaving it with a sense of relief is an obvious example of the 'homophily' promoted by social media: 'individuals' propensity to cluster based on common traits, such as political ideology' (Barberà, 2020, p. 37). It is well-nigh impossible to know to what extent the virtual friendships and the sense of community with 'Shakespeare' at the centre that were a feature of the pandemic for many of the scholars in my network are a matter of conscious decisions about with whom to engage. They are probably in almost equal measure the result of the imperceptible algorithms that delimit the boundaries of our social experience, shape our worldviews and potentially exclude individuals, experiences and views that do not accord with ours but that would require us to reconsider our opinions. I am struck by the extent to which, on the whole, entering lockdown and shifting my social interactions online, while letting my professional interests overlap with my private friendships, with both converging on the figure of Shakespeare, led to an acceleration and amplification of a sense of like-mindedness that may not have been all that progressive, even as it brought joy and solace at a difficult time.

To what extent did the very focus on Shakespeare exclude communities that have fought the primacy of the colonial legacy with which this playwright is associated more than any other? In the year in which the other viral social media event was concerned with the murder of George Floyd and the #BlackLivesMatter movement, was focusing on Shakespeare in performance a comfortable but unethical choice to make? Where were the non-Western Shakespeare productions? What, if they had the time, leisure, means to do so, were people in the Global South watching and/or performing during their lockdowns? And within the United Kingdom, is there a connection between the predominance of Shakespeare in the British pandemic repertoire and the unemployment figures for performers that show that 'people of colour were more likely to leave' creative occupations than white artists (Mark Taylor in Centre for Cultural Value, 2021, 16.42)? While Shakespeare's plays, therefore, provided a cultural 'glue' that bound us together at times of the most intense crisis, provided the familiarity that made innovation commercially viable and a means of asserting the enduring value of art and culture, Shakespeare may also have accelerated existing trends that fuel social and political division.

That said, now that the viral threat is receding a little, Shakespeare is also somewhat fading out of the repertoire, and a more diverse set of voices is beginning to be heard. At Shakespeare's Globe, Michelle Terry is continuing her quiet revolution with a production of *Romeo and Juliet* that is socially distanced, racially diverse and progressive in its use of trigger warnings and a Brechtian framing that re-places Shakespeare's tragedy within the pandemic present of depression, emotional neglect and trauma. But old privileges and habits are hard to stamp out: Sir Ian McKellen has just starred in an 'age-blind' *Hamlet* in Windsor to socially distanced audiences: the language of equality is deployed to entrench the privileges of those unaffected by precarity. Even a global pandemic will not change some of the privileges of celebrity or the dominance of that particular play.

What the pandemic has changed for me, and for many of the other scholars writing about performance at this time, is our mode of writing. The criticism of productions watched in lockdown has, almost without exception, been remarkably personal, with writers bringing their private lives and contexts of viewing into the writing as naturally as we now share details of our home environments on our Zoom and Teams screens in meetings. Lockdown has forced introspection if simply because it has not been possible to carry out research in the more usual, supposedly objective, mode of writing underpinned by extensive archival and library research.

The result, for this Element, has been what I have called a phenomenological history of viewing Shakespeare in lockdown; I could also call it a form of autoethnography that uses my personal experience of pandemic theatregoing as its touchstone. Writing in this way may seem self-indulgent, but it felt more like a sometimes gruelling exercise in self-examination and honesty. It has forced an acknowledgement of positionality and privileges: good health, ability to go into self-isolation without economic threat, having a room of my own to work in, a screen of my own to watch on, reliable WiFi, shared childcare, access to a digital library, language skills, a workload I was able to adapt and so on. Writing in a pandemic requires a systematic un-learning of assumptions of objectivity, and an acknowledgement of affect and context as factors that profoundly colour what Shakespeare is, and means, at any one point, for any single person.

This is nothing new: Terence Hawkes years ago proclaimed that 'Shakespeare doesn't mean: *we* mean *by* Shakespeare' (1992, p. 3, emphasis in orignal), and Barbara Hodgdon (2021) famously grounded her foundational work in Shakespeare performance studies in her own somatic response to the productions she witnessed and the archival artefacts she handled. Yet what the pandemic seems to have brought about is an intensification and more wide-spread awareness of the need to bear witness to the events we are embroiled with. It has accentuated the tension between the individuality of our own experience and the knowledge that we are also part of a global phenomenon that unites us in a shared vulnerability that nevertheless affects us in radically unequal ways. This teaches us some important lessons as the pandemic crisis recedes and the climate crisis erupts into the foreground with renewed urgency.

For Shakespeare studies, this might well mean a turning point: a point where we, as individual scholars, have to stand by our own witness statements, acknowledge our limitations and positionality yet more openly than hitherto and also listen to the stories of people whose experiences and interests are profoundly dissimilar to ours. It means recognising that in these global crises, there is no uniformity: different countries, cities, communities, families, individuals are affected in profoundly different ways. Some of us might have been watching Shakespeare together, but that togetherness is strictly circumscribed, to a large extent fabricated, and needs to be unpicked yet further. That, in turn, necessitates an ethical recognition that our entrenched modes of organising the world and our activities within it – the very preoccupation with Shakespeare that seemed such an unproblematic source of joy and community – are underpinned by privileges that are not shared. As we emerge from the pandemic, should we more firmly question the role Shakespeare played in consolidating those privileges?

Is *this* the promised end? (*King Lear*, 5.3.237, emphasis added)

References

Aebischer, P. (2020). *Shakespeare, Spectatorship and the Technologies of Performance*. Cambridge: Cambridge University Press.

Aebischer, P. and Nicholas, R. (2020a). *Digital Theatre Transformation: A Case Study and Digital Toolkit*. Oxford: Creation Theatre. http://hdl.handle.net/10871/123464

Aebischer, P. and Nicholas, R. (2020b). Digital Theatre Transformation_Audience Questionnaire_anon.xlsx. figshare. Dataset. https://doi.org/10.6084/m9.figshare.13076963.v1

Allred, G. K. (2022, forthcoming). Notions of Liveness in Lockdown Shakespeare. In Allred, G. K., Broadribb, B. and Sullivan, E., eds. *Shakespeare in Lockdown: New Evolutions in Performance and Adaptation*. London: Bloomsbury.

Allred, G. K. and Broadribb, B. (2022a, forthcoming). Case Study: Introducing Big Telly. In G. K. Allred, Broadribb, B. and Sullivan, E., eds. *Shakespeare in Lockdown: New Evolutions in Performance and Adaptation*. London: Bloomsbury.

Allred, G. K. and Broadribb, B. (2022b, forthcoming). Lockdown Shakespeare: A (Long) Year in Review. In G. K. Allred, Broadribb, B. and Sullivan, E., eds. *Shakespeare in Lockdown: New Evolutions in Performance and Adaptation*. London: Bloomsbury.

Backscheider, P. R., ed. (1992). *Daniel Defoe: Journal of the Plague Year*. New York: Norton.

Bakhtin, M. (1984). *Rabelais and His World*. Trans. by Helene Iswolsky. Bloomington: Indiana University Press.

Bakhshi, H., Mateos-Garcia, J. and Throsby, D. (2010). *Beyond Live: Digital Innovation in the Performing Arts*. London: NESTA (Research Briefing), https://media.nesta.org.uk/documents/beyond_live.pdf

Barberà, P. (2020). Social Media, Echo Chambers, and Political Polarization. In N. Persily and J. A. Tucker, eds. *Social Media and Democracy: The State of the Field, Prospects for Reform*. Cambridge: Cambridge University Press, pp. 34–55. Open Access web publication.

Barnett, D. (2014). Heiner Müller, *Die Hamletmaschine*. In P. W. Marx, ed. *Hamlet-Handbuch: Stoffe, Aneignungen, Deutungen*. Stuttgart: Verlag J. B. Metzler, pp. 422–8.

Bernard, J. F. (2019). Hamlet's Story/Stories of Hamlet: Shakespeare's Theater, the Plague, and Contagious Storytelling. In Darryl Chalk and Mary Floyd-Wilson, eds. *Contagion and the Shakespearean Stage*. Cham, Switzerland: Palgrave Macmillan, pp. 213–32.

Betancourt, M. (2017). *Glitch Art in Theory and Practice: Critical Failures and Post-Digital Aesthetics*. New York: Routledge.

Bizzocchi, J. (2009). The Fragmented Frame: The Poetics of the Split-Screen. Media-in-Transition 6 Conference – Stone and Papyrus, Storage and Transmission, 24–26 April 2009. Cambridge, MA. http://web.mit.edu/comm-forum/mit6/papers/Bizzocchi.pdf

Bloom, G. (2018). *Gaming the Stage: Playable Media and the Rise of English Commercial Theater*. Ann Arbor: University of Michigan Press.

Bogost, I. (2010). I Became a Fan of Marshall McLuhan on Facebook and Suggested that You Become a Fan, Too. In D. E. Wittkower, ed. *Facebook and Philosophy: What's on Your Mind?* Chicago, IL: Open Court, pp. 21–32.

Borzuk, A. (2021). Review: *The Duchess of Malfi* (Online). *Exeunt Magazine*, 18 March 2021, http://exeuntmagazine.com/reviews/review-duchess-malfi-online/

Broadribb, B. (2021a). 'Peace! The Charm's Wound Up': Subverting Virtual Theatre in Big Telly's Macbeth and Hijinx Theatre's Metamorphosis. *'Action is Eloquence': Rethinking Shakespeare*. Blog post, 2 January, https://medium.com/action-is-eloquence-re-think

ing-shakespeare/peace-the-charms-wound-up-subverting-virtual-thea
tre-in-big-telly-s-macbeth-and-hijinx-15b01f5488d2

Broadribb, B. (2022, forthcoming). Lockdown Screen Adaptation and the Metamodern Sensibility. In G. K. Allred, Broadribb, B. and Sullivan, E., eds. *Shakespeare in Lockdown: New Evolutions in Performance and Adaptation.* London: Bloomsbury.

Broadribb, B. (2021b, forthcoming). *Macbeth* (Review). *Shakespeare Bulletin* 39.2.

Brown, J. R. (1993). Foreign Shakespeare and English-Speaking Audiences. In D. Kennedy, ed. *Foreign Shakespeare: Contemporary Performance.* Cambridge: Cambridge University Press, pp. 21–35.

Buchanan, J. and Wyver, J. (2020). The Arts in Lockdown. YouTube: TORCH: The Oxford Research Centre in the Humanities, https:// www.youtube.com/watch?v=DLw0du1sKQI

Butler, J. (2021). Bodies That Still Matter. In A. Halsema, K. Kwastek and R. van den Oever, eds. *Bodies That Still Matter.* Amsterdam: Amsterdam University Press, pp. 177–93.

Centre for Cultural Value (2021). Webinar: Covid-19: 'The Great Unequaliser?' *Culture Hive.* 12 March. www.culturehive.co.uk/ CVIresources/webinar-covid-19-the-great-unequaliser/

Clarke, E. (2020). Stay Alert Memes: 18 Reactions that Sum Up How Confused Some People Are. *Evening Standard*, 11 May 2020, https://www.standard .co.uk/news/uk/stay-alert-memes-boris-johnson-lockdown-update-a4436921.html

Clubb, L. G. (1989). *Italian Drama in Shakespeare's Time.* New Haven, CT: Yale University Press.

Cook, A. (2009). Wrinkles, Wormholes and 'Hamlet': The Wooster Group's 'Hamlet' as a Challenge to Periodicity. *TDR/The Drama Review* 53(4): 104–19.

Costley, D. (2020). Zoom's Virtual Background Feature Isn't Built for Black Faces. *OneZero*, 26 October, https://onezero.medium.com/zooms-virtual-background-feature-isn-t-built-for-black-faces-e0a97b591955#:~:text=A%20scientist%20warns%20that%20bias,false%20arrests%2C%20lost%20job%20opportunities&text=Ainissa%20Ramirez%20says%20she's,a%20few%20times%20this%20year.&text=She%20pointed%20to%20the%20way,into%20the%20formula%E2%80%9D%20of%20film

Dasent, J. R., ed. (2009). *Acts of the Privy Council of England, New Series, Vol. XXIV, A. D. 1592–3*. Burlington, ONT: TannerRitchie Publishing.

Dekker, T. (1603). *The Wonderfull Yeare. 1603. Wherein Is Shewed the Picture of London, Lying Sicke of the Plague. At the Ende of All (Like a Mery Epilogue to a Dull Play) Certaine Tales Are Cut Out in Sundry Fashions, of Purpose to Shorten the Liues of Long Winters Nights, that Lye Watching in the Darke for Vs*. London: Thomas Creede. STC (2nd ed.) / 6535.3. Early English Books Online/ProQuest LLC.

Dennis, J. (2019). Creation Create a Hilarious After-Dark Adventure Comedy *Tempest* Where the Audience Are as Shipwrecked as the Cast, *Daily Info*, 24 July, www.dailyinfo.co.uk/feature/15426/the-tempest

Dickson. A. (2020). Shakespeare in Lockdown: Did He Write King Lear in Plague Quarantine? *The Guardian*, 22 March, https://www.theguardian.com/stage/2020/mar/22/shakespeare-in-lockdown-did-he-write-king-lear-in-plague-quarantine

Dobson, M. (2013). Foreign Shakespeare and the Uninformed Theatre-Goer. In S. Bennett and C. Carson, eds. *Shakespeare Beyond English: A Global Experiment*. Cambridge: Cambridge University Press, pp. 190–4.

Equity UK. (2020). Covid-19 Financial Support Guide. Equity.org.uk. 2 November, https://www.equity.org.uk/media/5543/covid-19-financial-support-guide_-v21.pdf

Fetzer, T. (2020). Subsidising the Spread of Covid19: Evidence from the UK's Eat-Out-to-Help-Out Scheme. *The Economic Journal*, https://academic.oup.com/ej/advance-article/doi/10.1093/ej/ueab074/6382847

Gillinson, M. (2020). The Tempest Review – Interactive Online Production Goes Down a Storm. *The Guardian* (online), 12 April, https://www.theguardian.com/stage/2020/apr/12/the-tempest-review-interactive-online-zoom

Girard, R. (1974). The Plague in Literature and Myth. *Texas Studies in Literature and Language* 15(4): 833–50.

Hawkes, T. (1992). *Meaning by Shakespeare*. London and New York: Routledge.

Hodgdon, B. C. (2021). *Ghostly Fragments: Essays on Shakespeare and Performance*. Eds. Richard Abel and Peter Hollland. Ann Arbor: University of Michigan Press

Ingold, T. (2007). *Lines: A Brief History*. Abingdon: Routledge.

Kidnie, M. J. (2018). The Stratford Festival of Canada: Mental Tricks and Archival Documents in the Age of NTLive. In P. Aebischer, S. Greenhalgh and L. Osborne, eds. *Shakespeare and the 'Live' Theatre Broadcast Experience*. London: Bloomsbury (The Arden Shakespeare), pp. 133–46.

Kirwan, P. and Sullivan, E. (2020). From the Editors of the Special Reviews Section: Shakespeare in Lockdown. *Shakespeare Bulletin* 38(3): 1–5.

Knowles, R. (2004). *Reading the Material Theatre*. Cambridge: Cambridge University Press.

Lachmann, R. (1988–9). Bakhtin and Carnival: Culture as Counter-Culture. Trans. R. Eshelman and M. Davis. *Cultural Critique* 11: 115–52.

Lafferty, E. (2019). *The Tempest*: Creation Theatre Magic Brought to Shakespearean Classic. *Oxford Magazine*, www.oxmag.co.uk/articles/the-tempest/

Lambert, H. et al. (2020). COVID-19 as Global Challenge: Towards an Inclusive and Sustainable Future. *The Lancet: Planetary Health*. 4: e312–e14.

Lehmann, H.-T. (2006). *Postdramatic Theatre*. Trans. K. Jürs-Munby. London: Routledge.

Liedke, H. L. (2020). *The Tempest* (2020) by Creation Theatre: Live in Your Living Room. *Miranda* 21, n.p., https://journals.openedition.org/miranda/28323

Liedke, H. L. and Pietrzak-Franger, M. (2021). Viral Theatre: Preliminary Thoughts on the Impact of the COVID-19 Pandemic on Online Theatre. *Journal of Contemporary Drama in English* 9(1): 128–44.

Mitchell, L. (2019). Interview with Creation Theatre Company. BBC Radio Oxford, 13 July, www.facebook.com/CreationTheatre/videos/the-tempest-rehearsals-on-bbc-radio-oxford/443882296448706/

Mori, M. ([1970]2012). The Uncanny Valley: The Original Essay by Masahiro Mori. Trans. K.F. MacDorman and N. Kageki. Originally published in Japanese in *Energy* 7.4, pp. 33-35, 1970. *IEEE Spectrum*, 12 June, https://spectrum.ieee.org/the-uncanny-valley

Müller, H. (2001a). *Die Hamletmaschine*. In F. Hörnigk, ed. *Heiner Müller: Werke 4: Stücke 2*. Berlin: Suhrkamp Verlag, pp. 545–54.

Müller, H. (2001b). *The Hamletmachine, by Heiner Mueller, 1979*. Trans. D. Redmond. theater.augent.be/file/13.

Müller, H. (2012). Shakespeare: A Difference. In C. Weber and P. D. Young, trans. *Heiner Müller After Shakespeare*. New York: PAJ Publications, pp. 172–5.

Nahon, K. and Hemsley, J. (2013). *Going Viral*. Cambridge: Polity Press.

NESTA. (2010). 'Beyond Live: Digital Innovation in the Performing Arts,' Research Briefing, February 2010. www.nesta.org.uk/sites/default/files/beyond_live.pdf

Parker-Starbuck, J. (2009). The Play-within-the-film-within-the-play's the Thing: Re-Transmitting Analogue Bodies in the Wooster Group's

Hamlet. *International Journal of Performance Arts and Digital Media* 5(1): 23–34.

Phelan, P. (1993). *Unmarked: The Politics of Performance*. London: Routledge.

Raber, K. (2018). *Shakespeare and Posthumanist Theory*. London: Bloomsbury (The Arden Shakespeare).

Raines, K. (2020). Act 2: National Audience Research: Wave 2: 22 June – 15 July 2020. Indigo-Ltd. http://s3-eu-west-1.amazonaws.com/super cool-indigo/Act-2-Report-wave-2-results.pdf

Reijn, H. and Wilson, R. (2018). Playing Female Roles in the Classics: Halina Reijn and Ruth Wilson, in conversation (June 2017). In S. Bennett and S. Massai, eds., *Ivo Van Hove: From Shakespeare to David Bowie*. London: Methuen, pp. 33–8.

Ristani, M. (2020). Theatre and Epidemics: An Age-Old Link. *Critical Stages/Scènes Critiques* 21. June, www.critical-stages.org/21/theatre-and-epidemics-an-age-old-link/#:~:text=First%20of%20all%20we%20must,a%20delirium%20and%20is%20communicative.&text=The%20present%20analysis%20is%20an,anxiety%20to%20fascination%20and%20influence.

Rogoff, Gordon. (1986). Hamletmaschine by Heiner Müller and Robert Wilson. *Performing Arts Journal* 10(1): 54–7.

Sample, I. and Davis, N. (2020). Covid Cases Among Secondary School-Aged Children Rise in England. *The Guardian*, 2 October, www.theguar dian.com/world/2020/oct/02/covid-cases-among-secondary-school-aged-children-rise-in-england

Schneider, R. (2001), 'Performance Remains', *Performance Research* 6(2): 100–108.

Shakespeare, W. (1832). *Hamlet*. Trans. A. W. von Schlegel. Gütersloh: Sigbert Mohn Verlag, pp. 581–688. Projekt Gutenberg, www.projekt-gutenberg.org/shakespr/hamlet-s/hamlet-s.html

Shakespeare, W. (1997). *The Norton Shakespeare*, 3rd ed., S. Greenblatt et al., eds. New York and London: W. W. Norton.

Shaughnessy, R. (2020). *About Shakespeare: Bodies, Spaces and Texts*. Cambridge: Cambridge University Press.

Shellard, D. (2004). Economic Impact Study of UK Theatre. London: Arts Council England, www.researchgate.net/publication/265004678_Economic_impact_study_of_UK_theatre

Smith, P. J., Valls-Russell, J. and Yabut, D. (2020). Shakespeare under Global Lockdown: Introduction. *Cahiers Élisabéthains* 103 (1): 101–11.

Sullivan, E. (2018a). The Audience Is Present: Aliveness, Social Media, and the Theatre Broadcast Experience. In P. Aebischer, S. Greenhalgh and L. Osborne, eds. *Shakespeare and the 'Live' Theatre Broadcast Experience*. London: Bloomsbury (The Arden Shakespeare), pp. 59–75.

Sullivan, E. (2018b). The Role of the Arts in the History of Emotions: Aesthetic Experience and Emotion as Method. *Emotions: History, Culture, Society* 2: 113–31.

Sullivan, E. (2022, forthcoming). Conclusion. In G. K. Allred Broadribb, B. and Sullivan, E., eds. *Shakespeare in Lockdown: New Evolutions in Performance and Adaptation*. London: Bloomsbury.

Templeman, S. (2013). 'What's this? Mutton?': Food, Bodies, and Inn-Yard Performance Spaces in Early Shakespearean Drama. *Shakespeare Bulletin* 31(1): 79–94.

United Nations. (2020). Countries Urged to Act against COVID-19 'Infodemic'. *UN News*, 23 September. https://news.un.org/en/story/2020/09/1073302

Van Hove, I. (2018). The Taming of the Shrew: Ivo van Hove (Extract from the Director's Notes). In S. Bennett and S. Massai, eds., *Ivo Van Hove: From Shakespeare to David Bowie*. London: Methuen, pp. 46–8.

Weimann, R. (1978). *Shakespeare and the Popular Tradition in the Theater*, trans. Robert Schwartz. Baltimore, MD: Johns Hopkins University Press.

West, W. N. (2006). Understanding in the Elizabethan Theatres. *Renaissance Drama, n.s.* 35: 113–43.

Worthen, W. B. (2003). *Shakespeare and the Force of Modern Performance*. Cambridge: Cambridge University Press.

Worthen, W. B. (2010). *Drama: Between Poetry and Performance*. Chichester, UK: Wiley-Blackwell.

Worthen, W. B. (2020). *Shakespeare, Technicity, Theatre*. Cambridge: Cambridge University Press.

Acknowledgements

This Element was written in isolation in my home office – but surrounded and carried by a community who kept me virtual company. Peter Kirwan's and Tom Cornford's early nudges got me going. Andrea Peghinelli's invitation to virtual Rome gave me a further push, and Keir Elam's encouragement removed a mental block. My parents and sister took over domestic duties so I could revise the Element.

Friends, colleagues and students old and new sustained me during this period. They organised and joined watch parties, Zoom discussions, research seminars; they shared resources and work-in-progress; they pointed me in the right direction, wrote blogs, commissioned reviews, exchanged ideas in seminars and brokered introductions that opened doors. They are Amber Ash, Michael Bartelle, Sonia Beard, Emily Bennett, Coco Brown, Judith Buchanan, Thea Buckley, Mark Burnett, Tom Cartelli, Robin Craig, Callan Davies, Anne-Valérie Dulac, Susannah Eig, Chris Ewers, Colette Gordon, Susanne Greenhalgh, Stuart Hampton-Reeves, Ronan Hatfull, Alex Heeney, Matthias Heim, Kelsey Jacobson, Elizabeth Jeffery, Peter Kirwan, Hester Lees-Jeffries, Michelle Manning, Sonia Massai, Harry McCarthy, Emer McHugh, Finn O'Riordain, Paul Prescott, Eoin Price, Stephen Purcell, Eleanor Rycroft, Robert Shaughnessy, Stephanie Shirilan, Connor Spence, Isabel Stuart, Holger Syme, Lyn Tribble, Rachel Willie, Ramona Wray, Laura Wright, John Wyver and the members of the #EuropeanTheatreClub. Erin Sullivan stands out as a source of inspiration and strength, and Gemma Allred, Benjamin Broadribb and Rachael Nicholas as fellow travellers. Coen Heijes saved me with Dutch translations and explanations. Former PhD students Harry McCarthy, Jim Porteous, Sally Templeman and Callan Davies extended my horizons and influenced my thinking about theatregrams, meshworks, somatic empathy, and *The Tempest*..

I have been in awe of the creative practitioners who have kept going this year and have kept others going by doing so. Creation Theatre's Lucy Askew is a generous, creative force for good. Zoë Seaton sparks joy with every show. Warm thanks, too, to the other wonderful creatives and staff behind *The Tempest* (2020): Al Barclay, Ryan Duncan, Rhodri Lewis, Madeleine McMahon, Charlie Morley, Crissy O'Donovan, Sinéad Owens, Stephen Spencer-Hyde, Giles Stoakley, PK Taylor, Annabelle Terry, Emily Walsh. Patrick Flick invited me to STA meetings and Robert Myles and Sarah Peachey provided precious insights into The Show Must Go Online (apologies for not writing more about their work here).

Section 2 of this book draws on the AHRC-funded *Digital Theatre Transformation: A Case Study and Digital Toolkit for Small to Mid-Scale Theatres in England* project on which I worked with Rachael Nicholas, who has been brilliant in every way. A short segment of the material on *The Tempest* is adapted from the chapter co-authored with Rachael on 'Creation Theatre and Big Telly's *The Tempest*: Digital Theatre and the Performing Audience' (Allred, Broadribb and Sullivan, 2022, forthcoming).

My sincere thanks to Emily Hockley and Bill Worthen, who believed in the project from the start and have offered only encouragement and patience when it was delayed, one lockdown and Covid-19 project at a time. The readers of this Element were generous and had brilliant advice to offer. Thank you, too, to Clay Hapaz, Richard Budd, arno declair, Maddie Dai, Lucy Askew, Crissy O'Donovan, Schauspielhaus Bochum, Femke de Veer and Joris van den Ring-Bax on behalf of ITA, for image permissions.

Finally, my deepest thanks go to my family: David Jones, Rhiannon and Glyn, who flapped their arms in unison with me when watching *The Tempest*. I could not have wished for a more funny, sensitive, tolerant, clever and kind group of always interesting individuals to be locked down with.

In memory of Gareth, Aimée, Catherine.

Cambridge Elements ☰

Shakespeare Performance

W. B. Worthen
Barnard College

W. B. Worthen is Alice Brady Pels Professor in the Arts, and
Chair of the Theatre Department at Barnard College. He is also
co-chair of the Ph.D. Program in Theatre at Columbia
University, where he is Professor of English and Comparative
Literature.

ABOUT THE SERIES

Shakespeare Performance is a dynamic collection in a field that is both always emerging and always evanescent. Responding to the global range of Shakespeare performance today, the series launches provocative, urgent criticism for researchers, graduate students and practitioners. Publishing scholarship with a direct bearing on the contemporary contexts of Shakespeare performance, it considers specific performances, material and social practices, ideological and cultural frameworks, emerging and significant artists and performance histories

Cambridge Elements $\equiv$

Shakespeare Performance

Printed in the United States
by Baker & Taylor Publisher Services